Bishop Carrie J. Surratt

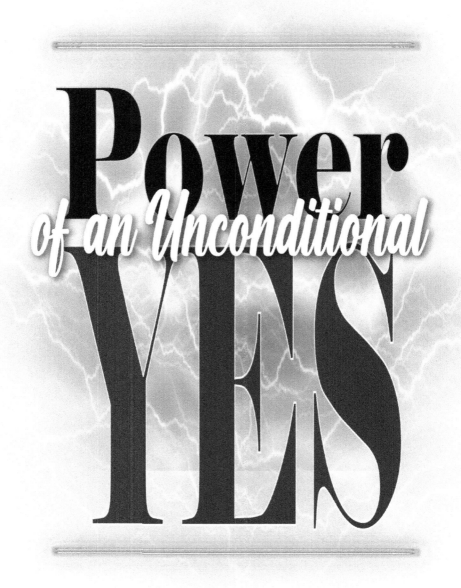

Printed in the United States
Published by Harrod Publishing LLC

Power Of An Unconditional Yes
Bishop Carrie J. Surratt

ISBN 978-0-9997275-9-1

TABLE OF CONTENTS

This book is dedicated to
ELDER DEBORAH ANN COLEMAN

Elder Deborah was a faithful Elder in the Lord's Church and a dear, loyal friend of forty plus years. She went home to glory in the middle of the night January 11, 2022.

She faithfully encouraged me to write and consistently prayed for and with me regarding my writing projects.

Elder Deborah was an anointed vessel full of wisdom, a devoted teacher of the word, an effective soul winner, and a loyal servant who had given God an unconditional yes. She is missed sorely!

ACKNOWLEDGEMENTS

It is with sincere thankfulness and appreciation that I acknowledge my writing coach, Dr. Latonia Valincia Moss, who has taught me how to write a book. She planted words of encouragement in me that removed all apprehensions about completing this writing project. While coaching me in writing and reading the draft, the anointing of Holy Spirit moved upon her, He brought change, restoration, and healing in her life.

Absolutely, Dr. Moss is the perfect individual to craft the foreword of this book, which is her testimony of the power within these pages. Thank you for the long sessions on zoom, and for your persistence to meet even while you were painfully recovering from surgery. You are an amazing, proficient, and dynamite teacher, and you are my incredible writing coach. Thank you!

I acknowledge the joy of my life, my daughter Tina Surratt, for always being available to assist me with technical difficulties, answering questions and for tolerating my moments of frustration. Moreover, I am overwhelmingly appreciative for the prophetic song Tina wrote after being inspired by the sermon "Unconditional Yes". I have included the words of the song in the introduction.

I gratefully acknowledge family! Verta Larkins was my most faithful encourager. She was consistent in praying for me personally, praying for the writing project, and she often gave me a prophetic word of encouragement.

I appreciate Adrianne Lawrence, who has a servant's heart. There were many days I would write for long hours, leaving no time for family duties or home chores. Adrianne willingly filled the gap preparing many delicious meals for the family in my stead; as well as, taking care of things around the house.

Finally, I acknowledge the intercessors of The Lord's Church of Restoration and thank each of them for diligently and effectively interceding on my behalf. I love them and am blessed by their love and support.

FOREWORD

With over twenty years as an Elder in Christianity, I liken Bishop Carrie Surratt to a prophetic curate. She has penned a book as a divine panacea to cure broken and weary souls. Bishop Surratt exegetes a three-letter word, "yes" and its power when affixed to an unconditional assent. Bishop Surratt, a garden of knowledge with over forty years of expertise, experiences, and education in Christendom, authored this book—Power of an Unconditional Yes. It is a clarion call to ascend to the powers an unconditional yes offers believers.

Bishop Surratt inspires us to reconsider our relationships with the Most Holy One, to deconstruct and repurpose our understanding of the Bible, to take a litmus test to determine where we are in our walk with God. We get to reacquaint ourselves with God's love, the foundation of Christianity. Bishop Surratt delivers pictures of God's ubiquitous love in ocean size proportions. Reading through the pages, I found myself relishing in God's love as if a famished infant. She wrote and grabbed my heartstrings with each word as if God was mending my broken soul with tenderness and affection. I wept while reading about the possibility of restoration and renewed faith in my Christian life. I was cured of being a Christian on autopilot with all the years of judging my experiences from a trauma-based mindset.

I was given an opportunity to explore the definition of unconditional yes and the power and the benefits of giving God a yes. There is POWER available to believers. Bishop Surratt used scriptures and her own 40 years of experience as a teacher/preacher in Christianity to prove it. The powers that were dormant in my life were kindled through this book. The book became an intense Bible study. There were promises in the scriptures that I had not leveraged. I did not have to rely on yesterday's manna for survival, this book was fresh milk, honey, and meat to my hopes, and my dreams that I had become too tired to be accomplished. Too overwhelmed to consider anymore, I found restless contentment in surviving life.

Power of an Unconditional Yes reignited my spiritual disciplines too. I stopped living off yesterday's glory because my "yes" was flaccid. My prayers half-hearted. I had been a robust intercessor, I loved to pray for anyone and about anything at the drop of a dime, I prayed. I had grown lackluster in my prayer life forgetting that prayer was more than intercession, but my own intimacy with God. Through these pages, I was reminded of the importance of consistency and necessity of prayer. The act of worship as a daily opportunity to commune with God, and other spiritual disciplines reimagined that had shrunk behind the grief and the worry of uncertain times were reignited.

Moreover, Power of an Unconditional Yes eloquently written, power-packed with scriptural proof of God's love and the harvest we can expect from trusting in him with an unconditional yes forced me to dig deeper in my relationship with Holy Spirit as a leader in Christianity. Being a leader and preacher did not stop the cloud of depression that overwhelmed me. Grief delivered such an unfamiliar sadness I had not known to this magnitude. Death was everywhere. I had probably been to ten funerals during this pandemic, eulogizing my mother and a beloved sister-in-Christ. My mother died while my health was declining, and the world was in such a flux of uncertainty. She died at the beginning of the year and my sister bookended that year dying from COVID-19. The New Year started with me testing positive for COVID-19. There was no symptom that escaped me. I questioned everything about my faith in God as death and fear surrounded me.

Nonetheless, this book provided hope again. It was not rhetoric or words that sat on the surface of my heart. It was hope packed in the powers this book promises to deliver. It gave me that mustard seed faith to believe again. It was a jolt to assuage the fears and apprehension about life and allowed me to reimagine an unconditional yes! For many of us, we have lost hope and become disillusioned with religion that we forgot that God is not the people, God did not create our messes, God is not the pandemic, God is our refuge. God is the love through the atrocities of life. Experiences are what life is made of and we have assigned judgments to those experiences and then have our requisite pity party to assure us that we are not enough, or unlove, or cursed, or whatever is our human answer to suffering. I was reminded that giving God an unconditional yes is still a necessary response to whatever is happening, whatever experiences lie at the door.

Power of an Unconditional Yes, became my testimony. I was encouraged. I took the advice on the pages and utilized them. I relied on God's powers while daily practicing the dedicated disciplines that honored my unconditional yes. I reminded myself daily of the powers that are available to me through relationship with Holy Spirit. I am hopeful that after reading this book believers feel motivated and equipped to say, "yes," and say it unconditionally remembering (adopted from the Message Bible - Ephesians 3:20) God can do anything—far more than we could ever imagine or guess or request in our wildest dreams! He does it not by pushing us around but by working within us, his Spirit deeply and gently within us." And all that requires is an unconditional yes!

Dr. Latonia Valincia Moss

INTRODUCTION

M y first spiritual experience took place at the tender age of twelve years old; and two years later, I was saved and received the in-filling of the Holy Spirit. My Mother and Pastor were both devoted praying women who helped to lay my foundation in prayer, faith, and God's Word. They taught me to have faith and pray, to live holy, to submit to the Lord, to love Him, and to always obey Him.

I was eager to learn all I could about this wonderful God who has saved me and was faithful to adhere to the foundational teachings I received in church and at home. I believe my mother knew God had a plan for my life. She said to me several times, "Carrie Jean, you must live holy for God to use you, and you must always say yes to the Lord." At age sixteen, I gave the Lord my first yes when He called me by name to preach His Word.

During the following two years of studying and training to preach, I experienced the tremendous and life-changing power of yes and Holy Spirit. The little store-front church I attended needed a musician and I cried out to the Lord to anoint me to be able to render music for the services. I prayerfully prepared a petition asking the Lord to anoint me and teach me how to play the piano. While I was in prayer, the Lord asked me if I was willing to fast and pray when I presented the petition to Him; and my quick response to Him was "Yes Lord". My yes was unconditional, because I did not know the stipulations, instructions or duration of the fast.

I was instructed to fast food and water for seven days and nights, and to pray three times a day. My Pastor and Mom were my encouragers who prayed with me during the week. I attended high school five days and had a part-time job in a beauty shop three days of my seven-day fast. I was physically weak by day four, which was a school day and a workday. Nonetheless, I was determined to keep my agreement with the Lord, because I knew He would answer my petition with power and demonstration.

Holy Spirit was my Teacher and my Helper as I sat on the scraggily bench in front of the piano that was not perfectly tuned and had some broken keys. A miracle happened! I was empowered and anointed by Holy Spirit with musical ability and comprehension. It was a profound experience with new dimensions of God's power as He taught me what a cord was, and that there were three major cords to every key. Moreover, I was instructed to learn the three major cords in every key, because that would give me the ability and capability to play any song. Understand, the miracle took place from the submission of an unconditional yes and Holy Spirit activated various dimensions of God's power in my life.

I came to the realization and revelation that the tiny word yes was extremely powerful when I began to study and prepare a sermon titled: "Unconditional Yes". The scripture text was II Corinthian 1:20-21a, from The Message Bible says: "Whatever God has promised gets stamped with the Yes of Jesus. In him, this is what we preach and pray, the great Amen, God's Yes and our Yes together, gloriously evident. God affirms us, making us a sure thing in Christ, putting his Yes within us." The scripture alone was so powerful, it stirred a deep desire within me to seek revelation knowledge about yes. The sermon was about the power of God that would be released from the submission of an unconditional yes to different levels of God's power.

After having preached the sermon a number of times, my quest to know and understand the action of yes intensified. As I studied and researched the word yes and the power activity attached to it, I also practiced and activated the principles of the sermon in my life by giving the Lord an unconditional yes. I witnessed the release of supernatural power, ability, and strength, magnificent deliverances, and extraordinary miracles. Holy Spirit activated various dimensions of God's power in my life as I continued to say yes to His word, His will, and His way.

Finally, the Lord empowered my daughter Tina, to write a prophetic song from the sermon "Unconditional Yes". The song eloquently summarizes the cause and effect of giving a yes to the Lord.

THE SONG: Yes Lord,

Yes will propel you into your destiny,

Commitment to His way, His Work, and His Word will set you free.

God is watching and He is waiting for an answer from you,

Will it be yes, yes, yes Lord?

He is expecting your yes,

The Lord will accept and accomplish your yes,

He will maintain and bless your yes.

Yes, Yes, Yes, Yes, Yes Lord!

The power of an unconditional yes has worked over and over in my life and in my ministry. Therefore, be encouraged to read and study the compilation of information and principles within these pages! Be encouraged to study, pray, and practice the principles, and the teachings of Holy Spirit. This book will break down the powers that an unconditional yes supports and great blessings will follow.

Chapter One

LOVE FOUNDATION

*Let everything you do be done in love [motivated and inspired by God's
love for us. I Corinthians 16:14 (AMP)*

*I have loved you even as the Father has loved me. Live within my
love. When you obey me, you are living in my love, just as I obey my
Father and live in his love. John 15: 9-10 (Living Bible)*

QUESTIONS:

- What's love got to do with it?
- What's love got to do with, yes?
- What's love got to do with an unconditional, yes?
- The answer is EVERYTHING!

L ove is the most magnificent force mankind has ever
experienced and is the greatest force in the earth. Most
importantly, love is the foundation of God's relationship with
humanity; wherein, He exercises and expresses His goodness,
generosity, benevolence, and intimate passion for His creation
mankind. God loves us, He has plans for our lives, and He has
chosen us to be His own! The greatest expression of God's

love is the gifts of His dear son. How awesomely true it is, God so loved the world that He gave His Son to die that we might live! God's love for us is extensive, the height, the breadth, and the depth of His love is far reaching. The scripture that verbalizes the greatest example of God's love is John 3:16 (AMP) which reads, "For God so [greatly] loved and dearly prized the world, that He [even] gave His [One and] only begotten Son, so that whoever believes and trusts in Him [as Savior] shall not perish but have eternal life." God so dearly prized His creation, and profoundly loved humanity that He gave life to us through the death of His son Jesus.

The definition of love (agape` Greek) is to love, cherish, esteem; also, it means loyalty, respect, prize, relish accept and be devoted to. We see God's love for man in 1John 3:1(NIV), "See what great love the Father has lavished on us, that we should be called children of God! And that is what we are! The reason the world does not know us is that it did not know him." We are esteemed, relished, and cherished by God; that is exciting! For He so loved and predestined us to be His own and designed a plan of redemption for us. God's giving is the personification of unconditional love, furthermore it is unrestricted, unlimited, and unreserved love. God chose us, He preferred us, personally handpicked us, and predestined us to be His own despite our frailties, sins, shortcomings, or mistakes. Unequivocally, God is deserving of our agreement, attestation, and affirmation to His plan for us. God is God, He is Creator; therefore, we should willingly give Him a "Yes Lord" from a heart saturated with His love.

There is an abundance and overflow of God's love available to us. John 15: 9-10 (Living Bible) states: "I have loved you even as the Father has loved me. Live within my love. 10 When you obey me you are living in my love, just as I obey my Father and live in his love." How do we live in His love? We live in His love by acceptance and reciprocation. We accept His great love wherewith He loved us and love Him wholeheartedly in return. The above scripture gives us a deeper insight regarding living in God's love in the Passion Translation. "I love each of you with the same love that the Father loves me. You must continually let my love nourish your hearts. If you keep my commands, you will live in my love, just as I have kept my Father's commands, for I continually live nourished and empowered by His love." (John 15: 9-10) What a joy it is to live in His love, and to be nourished by it and be empowered by this great love of God!

Imperatively, the dynamic love foundation is a triad of oneness; and, the means by which we continually live in God's love. Jesus declared that His Father was in Him, and He was in His Father, and they would be in us. He also prayed that we would experience the endless flow of the Father's love and the power of oneness as He had experienced with his Father. This triad demonstrates complete unity, an abundance of love and profound oneness with the Father and the Son: moreover, it gives exuberant strength to the love foundation. The word says we are to do what the Lord requires: which is to fear Him, walk in His ways, love, and serve him with all our heart and soul. (Deuteronomy 10:12) With a firm and unshakable love foundation, we will submit an obedient yes to His word and enjoy living in His love.

The greatest commandment in Matthew 22: 37-38 tells us to love the Lord with every passion of our heart, with all the energy of our being, and with every thought that is within. We can obey this supreme command because God himself has freely shared His love with us, equipping us to live continually in His love. Moreover, we live in His love by obeying His Word as Jesus did and by submitting to the Father's will. Our expression of love is returned to God and demonstrated when we agree, assent and give Him an "unconditional yes" to the following: 1) submit to the plan He has made for our lives, 2) yield to His Word by obedience, 3) trust his directions, and 4) follow His instructions. God has demonstrated His love for mankind profoundly, it should be our pleasure to love Him in return. Returned love to God is manifested when we submit, when we yield and when we trust His will, His way, and His word with an "unconditional yes".

Understand, God is love! He has equipped us to experience and enjoy love by pouring His love into the depths of our hearts. In Roman 5:5 (NCV) it reads: "And this hope will never disappoint us, because God has poured out his love to fill our hearts. He gave us his love through the Holy Spirit, whom God has given to us." This translation uses the word "poured" which deserves additional attention. The word signifies an enormous and free flowing amount of love has filled the core of our being. God, who is love, has poured himself and the knowledge of love into our inner most parts, flooding our hearts. A heart saturated with love by God equips us to respond to Him affirmatively, which is a "Yes Lord". We are prepared to reciprocate love through worship, obedience, solitude, and prayer without hesitation.

Knowing God is knowing love! It is imperative that we have a firm grasp of God's love and allow His love to operate in us, for us, and with us, which will bring the Lord pleasure. Understanding God's love and having increased knowledge of His love, will catapult us to obey the Lord, His Word, keep His commands, love Him, honor Him, and serve Him. Without question, God is deserving of our loyalty, devotion, allegiance, and obedience. Our love foundation must be solid, sure, and secure: as we are directed to follow the chartered course God has planned for us. Furthermore, we will be empowered from a love foundation into the deeper things of God, our purposes and destiny. The launching power is generated by the acceptance of His generous love and by submitting to His directions, instructions, His word, and continued guidance.

God loves us profoundly! Let us examine a few verses in the Book of Ephesians starting with Chapter one which expounds on His loving ownership. The Word clearly states the Lord has chosen, hand-picked us, and predestined us to be His own: He has repossessed, redeemed, regenerated, forgiven, and sealed us. Understand, this clearly identifies the great love relationship we have with our gracious and loving Father. He knows we are His since He has stamped his seal of love over our hearts and then gave us the Holy Spirit as a deposit guaranteeing our inheritance. Accepting and living in the Father's love, positions us to obey His word and to give Him an emphatic yes to His will.

God's love for us is awesome, astonishing, and astronomical! Several translations describe God's love as great, which means abundant and enormous. Ephesians 2:4-5 (AMP) states: "But God, being [so very] rich in mercy, because of His great and wonderful love with which He loved us, even when we were [spiritually] dead and separated from Him because of our sins, He made us [spiritually] alive together with Christ (for by His grace—His undeserved favor and mercy—you have been saved from God's judgment). It is because of His great love we have been raised and made to sit in the heavenly realm which is the center of God's operation; in addition, He activated His extensive love for us when He hand-picked us to be His very own. As we broaden our view and the depth of God's love, we will be inspired to new levels of obedience and will quickly submit an unconditional yes to our position in Him.

In Ephesians 3:17, we are encouraged to be rooted deep in God's love; this simply means to accept the resting place of His love deep in our hearts. The New Century Version says it very clearly for us: "I pray that Christ will live in your hearts by faith and that your life will be strong in love and be built on love." Our lives are built on a love foundation, wherein, we are rooted and grounded in His magnificent love. Beyond any doubt, our love foundation is secure in Jesus and as solid as a rock because of Jesus. The yes of Jesus was a saving yes for all humanity, by the shedding His sinless blood the price was paid for our redemption. And that's love! The expression of unconditional love has been demonstrated by Jesus through His life of honor, love, obedience, and submission to His Father.

Significantly, we must remain sensitive to the Father's voice to obey and submit to His promptings and return love to Him in everything. There must remain an acute awareness of His voice, regardless to how we hear him…. a small still voice, the voice in a vision, or a loud voice like thunder. We are compelled from a heart flooded with love to give God a "yes" when we hear His voice, a "yes" to His instructions and directions. God has reconciled and reclaimed us because we were His in the beginning; absolutely, He has a plan and purposes for the believers. Remember, He is our sovereign God, who is very much in control of our lives. Let me share my definition of sovereign which is: "God can do what He wants to, when He wants to, for whom He wants to, or not at all if He does not want to." He is the A and Z of everything, the ultimate in authority and rule, He is supreme, and He is sovereign. When He speaks, we hear and obey in love.

God in His infinite wisdom has provided several pathways that give us access to His abundant love, His presence, His power, and His will. The first pathway of access we will examine is in chapter two, known as dedicated disciplines. The practice of the disciplines will assist us to ascertain and acquired spiritual growth and development, which will enable us to easily give God an unconditional yes.

The disciplines are exercises we practice such as meditation and reflection on God's goodness, life-blessings, miracles and deliverances. Plus, we practice the dedicated disciplines of prayer, worship and celebration from a heart flooded with love for God, knowing the presence of love will create an atmosphere that will invoke the presence of the Lord.

Furthermore, the practice of the dedicated disciplines will expose us to the presence of the Lord, His mind and purpose for our lives, and teach us to yield to His power. The consistent practice of dedicated disciplines will assist us in the pursuit to ascertain and apprehend knowledge about our loving Father, moreover, solidify our love foundation and relationship by giving us a close walk with Him.

We will explore the tiny word "yes" in Chapter three and come to know it's wonderful worth, the power potentiality and love connection. What is the love connection? It is the profound love God demonstrated towards us by giving His only son to submit to death so we might live. In addition, it is the cascade of His love flooding our hearts to coagulate and congeal within to give unshakable strength to our love foundation. We will become well versed regarding the surrender of an unconditional yes, also, we will understand how to release God's power in our lives by the power of Holy Spirit.

The last essential pathway to be reviewed in this chapter is the promised Holy Spirit, the third person and power source of the Godhead. The love Jesus had for His followers and future believers was dynamic and commanding, wherein He promised to not leave us as orphans, but He would send another counselor. The promised Holy Spirit would come and has come to be our Helper, Counselor, Strengthener, Stand-By, Advocate, and Teacher. (John 15:26-27 AMP) He has come to be with us, upon us, and within us. Moreover, He is the Spirit of Truth, Spirit of Grace, Spirit of Faith, Spirit of Life, and the Spirit of Love working for our good. Holy Spirit is truth personified, giving us grace and faith for our journey, as He empowers us with the life of God and fills us with His unfailing love.

Provisionally, when draw near to God, giving Him an unconditional yes to His word, will, and way, we activate Holy Spirit who releases God's power in our lives. Various dimensions of God's power, from exousia to dynamia and dynamis, just to name a few, will be thoroughly identified and discussed in chapters four through seven. The information therein, will be extremely helpful to our spiritual maturity as it instructs us how to access the power of God. This pathway access with the assistance of Holy Spirit, will empower us to achieve, acquire, accomplish, and attain life goals, destiny, purpose, vision and dreams!

Importantly, the love foundation is impenetrable and secure because of the power of God's love. The return of our love to God flows obediently from a heart flooded with His love, and not from obligation. Unequivocally, love is something we do! We love wholeheartedly by submitting an unconditional yes to the Word and His will: therein, Holy Spirit will activate and release dimensions of God's power in our lives, as we practice the discipline and mature in the deeper things of God.

Chapter Two

DEDICATED DISCIPLINES

Study this Book of Instruction continually. Meditate on it day and night so you will be sure to obey everything written in it. Only then will you prosper and succeed in all you do. Joshua 1:8 (NLT)

Teach me, Lord, the way of your decrees, that I may follow it to the end. Give me understanding, so that I may keep your law and obey it with all my heart. Direct me in the path of your commands, for there I find delight. Psalm 119: 33-35 (NIV)

Our quest in life, as the beloved children of God should be to love Him and His Word, to worship and obey Him, work to succeed in purpose, and enjoy the blessings of being adopted into God's royal family. Understand, God has already deposited in us by His power, everything we need that pertains to life and godliness. It is our responsibility to utilize the vehicles of wisdom, and the avenues of knowledge that are available for our growth, development, transformation, and spiritual maturity.

There are several methods available to attain spiritual maturity, transformational growth, and development in the deeper things of God; the method we have chosen to use for spiritual maturity is the practice of dedicated disciplines. Oftentimes, this practice is referred to as spiritual disciplines, nevertheless, for the purpose of this discourse we identify them as dedicated disciplines and will expand on six of them in this chapter.

The word dedicated and its meaning gives a more accurate description of the selected practices that will be addressed. Dedicated means wholly committed or devoted to something, reserved for a specific purpose or personal goal. Discipline means training to act, activity; also, exercise and regimen that develops or improves skill. Moreover, dedicated disciplines are commitments to practice, train or exercise for personal improvement, relational advancement, spiritual maturity, and knowledge enhancement.

The disciplines will draw us nearer and expose us to God's Presence, illuminate dimensions and levels of His power, cultivate faith, and increase trust to be effectively anointed for ministry work. The consistent practice of these disciplines will solidify our spiritual foundation, empower us to successfully walk in the vocation wherewith we have been called, and further position us to say yes to the Lord as we yield and obey the promptings of Holy Spirit.

DEDICATED DISCIPLINES

The following are noteworthy characteristics of dedicated disciplines: 1) all disciplines have a biblical foundation, 2) they have been taught and modeled in the Bible, 3) they are intimate and personal, and 4) they are practices and activities, not attitudes. 1 Timothy 4: 7 (TPT) states: *"Be quick to abstain from senseless traditions and legends, but instead be engaged in the training of truth that brings righteousness."* The truth and transformational power of dedicated disciplines are not questioned, because they are all substantiated by the living and powerful word of God.

The disciplines are personal practices and activities; they are not acquired attitudes nor character qualities. In addition, they are more focused on doing than being, and should become a habit of holiness and devotion breeding spiritual improvement as we do them. The Bible will be our exercise manual for the disciplines. We have selected the following to expound upon: Study, Prayer, Worship, Meditation, Solitude, and Serving. Remember, they require activeness, exercise, animation, and movement, they are something we do consistently for our spiritual development and enhancement.

Dedicated Discipline 1

Study is a particular branch of learning and the acquisition of knowledge in a specific area. Studying the Word involves interpretation, observation, and application and is extremely beneficial to study in various translations of Scripture. When I practice the discipline of Study, I use five to seven different translations of Scripture to pulverize the verse or verses. Also, I use several different Bible Dictionaries to assist with the study. This dedicated discipline helps us to know God's ways, exposes us to His will, reveals His love, His sovereignty and His diverse powers to us.

In 2 Timothy 2:15, we are encouraged to: "Study and be eager and do your utmost to present yourself to God approved (tested by trial), a workman who has no cause to be ashamed, correctly analyzing, and accurately dividing [rightly handling and skillfully teaching] the Word of Truth." Studying the Word diligently will enhance our ability to rightly divide God's Word, moreover, it will increase our faith to obey and develop new trust levels for God and His Word.

The Bible also says in 2 Timothy 3:16-17 (ESV), "All Scripture is breathed out by God and profitable for teaching, for reproof, for correction, and for training in righteousness, that the man of God may be complete, equipped for every good work." Study by readings, confessing, declaring, memorizing, reciting, and pulverizing the Word. God watches over His word to perform it; His word will never return to Him unproductive, void, or unfulfilled. His word will always produce and accomplish what He desires. (Isaiah 55:11) Consistent study of God's word will enrich our lives and further prepare us for the work head. Study the word!

Dedicated Discipline 2

Prayer is an essential and effective spiritual vehicle by which we communicate and commune with God. It is intimate, heart-felt sharing with God our thoughts, desires and needs. Prayer is a dialogue, we talk, God listens, then God's speaks, we listen, we ask and God answers. In 1 John 5: 14-15 (NCV) "And this is the boldness we have in God's presence: that if we ask God for anything that agrees with what he wants, he hears us. If we know he hears us every time we ask him, we know we have what we ask from him." We pray according to His will and word; God hears and answers our prayers.

We have access to God through prayer, and according to James 5:16 the prayers of the righteous are powerful and effective. God's open door prayer policy is in Hebrews 4:16 (TPT) which says: "So now we come freely and boldly to where love is enthroned, to receive mercy's kiss and discover the grace we urgently need to strengthen us in our time of weakness." God is love and is enthroned waiting to hear our humble cry, the words of prayer, petitions, and supplications. The dedicated discipline of Prayer gives us access to God, when we pray, He will hear and answer our petitions with power and demonstration. Prayer is proactive and gives us a pathway to all the powers of Heaven for our earthly situations.

There are several postures for prayer, from kneeling, laying prostrate, to standing; however, the proclamation of the words of prayer are far more important than the posture we take when praying. Be encouraged to practice this discipline every day and many times throughout the day. The potentiality of prayer is far reaching, efficacious and effectual. According to Jeremiah 33:3 (ESV) "If we call on the Lord in prayer, He will answer and tell us great and hidden things that we have not known." The discipline of Prayer is loaded with possibilities and promises; it is the source of power placed in our lives to accomplish, to achieve and to attain knowledge and the blessings of His promises.

When we pray, fill the prayer with the living Word of God, because God watches over His Word to perform it. Also, when we pray, it is advantageous to pray in the spirit. The Bible says, "Pray passionately in the Spirit, as you constantly intercede with every form of prayer at all times." (Ephesians 6: 18b, TPT) and it also says pray in the spirit to build up our most holy faith. Praying in the spirit and in English are both powerful. When I practice the discipline of Prayer, I pray in the spirit for long periods of time. In fact, most of the time when I pray in tongues, I pray from one to three hours, praying to God with my heavenly language. This experience of praying in the spirit will build our most holy faith.

Demonstrate dedication and devotion to pray daily, because prayer activates and energies a reaching force of God's power. When we practice this dedicated discipline, it is the opportunity to communicate and converse with our Father. When we pray, it is our acceptance that God is our source, resource, and supply. Importantly, we pray promises in His word because prayer power will produce prayed promises.

Dedicated Discipline 3

Worship is another method available to us in accessing God, His presence, and His power. The Bible says in Psalm 95:6 (ESV) "Oh come, let us worship and bow down, let us kneel before the Lord, our Maker." Worship means reverent honor, adoring reverence, or regard. When we worship, admire, dote, and exalt the Lord, it summons His Presence. It is when His Presence is manifested among us that He brings presents, blessings, more love, peace, joy, strength, and ability.

Unrestricted worship is honoring and esteeming God with all our heart, soul, and mind. Unequivocally, worship is about the one we are worshipping, moreover, it flows from a heart of love and honor. God is exalted because He alone is the object of our worship. Psalm 29:2 tells us to ascribe to the Lord the glory due his name; worship the Lord in the splendor of holiness. It was in worship, when I first experience God's tangible glory which was like the dew of the morning. The more I adored Him, the more I exalted Him and appreciated His presence, the greater His presence was felt. When we pursuit the active presence of God, we become even more aware of His glory – the heavy laden, manifested Presence of God, with substances that satisfies. We ascribe adulation and audiation to Him for His greatness, moreover, when we worship, we accredit His magnification and exaltation to His Godness!

Grasp the truth of worship and do it! As we worship, we esteem His immensity and His infinity. Beyond any doubt, worship is a lifestyle of honor, adoration, and laudation to El Elyon, the Most High God. In Psalm 7:17 (ESV) it says: "I will give to the Lord the thanks due to his righteousness, and I will sing praise to the name of the Lord, the Most High." When practicing the discipline of Worship, we adore and highly esteem the Lord, kiss towards him, bow before him, reverently speak well of him, and His mighty acts. Engagement of the heart is essential when practicing the discipline of Worship. Oh, come let us adore Him! It is significant that our worship be accepted, received, and enjoyed by God. Our skill and talents are not weights for acceptance; our worship is only excellent because of Jesus. The major factors in acceptable worship are worship in the spirit, our union with Jesus and our faith in Him as Lord. Significantly, we must worship the Lord in the spirit of grace, truth, honor, and love. The discipline of Worship is extremely important and should be practiced daily, if possible. Every act of worship brings honor and appreciation to God who is love and who loves us unconditionally.

Dedicated Discipline 4

Meditation is continued thought, it is extended thought and contemplation. To meditate is to engage in thought for an uninterrupted and concentrated time. Meditation is a time to ponder or consider or about something. The Bible says our meditation should be pleasing to the Lord and we are to be glad in Him. Psalm 104:34.

I suggest a few steps of preparation be taken before beginning to avoid interruptions. These are steps I follow when I practice this discipline: 1) gather any needed materials, i.e., books, bibles, visual aids, and music, 2) select a comfortable seat, chair, or position, and 3) decide in advance how much time will be dedicated to meditating. I suggest you start with small blocks of time (2 or 4 minutes). Now, we quiet ourselves, center our minds, relax our breathing, and ask the Lord to be our guide.

I practice meditating silently or with words, thinking of His love, grace, and goodness. I invite the presence of the Lord in, ask Him to cover me, be pleased with my thoughts of Him, and allow me to enjoy His powerful presence. Meditating in silence is extremely rewarding to me. When experiencing this method of meditating, I see and speak mentally within. I allow my mind to see pictures or think of what I want to see, and my mind says what I am contemplating. It is extremely fulfilling when I experience deep and loving thoughts of my wonderful Lord.

As a dedicated discipline, meditation for believes is oftentimes mind-focused on the nuances of revealed truths, mainly the Word of God. In Joshua 1:8 (ESV) declares: "This Book of the Law shall not depart from your mouth, but you shall meditate on it day and night, so that you may be careful to do according to all that is written in it. For then you will make your way prosperous, and then you will have good success." The implication of meditate in this scripture is to ponder, imagine, mutter, study, and speak. The Message Bible says to ponder and meditate on the Word, and make sure to practice everything written in it. One of the most beneficial exercises of this discipline is to contemplate, think on, ponder, and speak a verse or a few verses of Scripture allowing it to soak into our mind, sink deep into our being and become alive in our spirit.

Amazingly, meditation does not stand alone, wherein, study, prayer and worship are active components of successful meditation. Many times, in our process we are praying and thinking, or worshipping as we reflect on the goodness of God. We are instructed in the Word of the Lord to meditate day and night, on His statues, on His precepts, His goodness, and His mighty acts. The Scripture says in Psalm 77:12 (NIV): "I will meditate on all your works and consider all your mighty deeds." Let's take a moment, meditate, and ponder on the wonderful hand of God and His mighty deeds! It is a blessing to draw His presence into our thought pattern and reflect on the wonders of His being and the power of His love.

Additionally, pulverizing is another form of meditation, it means to grind or reduce to dust or powder. To pulverize a scripture verse, we read or recite it verbatim several times, then change the wording but the meaning remains the same. Psalm 23:1 is a very familiar passage, The Lord is my shepherd, I shall not want. Let us grind it in our spirits by saying it aloud and differently each time.

My shepherd is my Lord
and I want for nothing.
I want for nothing because He is my shepherd.
Because the Lord is my shepherd
I always have all I need.
I do not want because the Lord is my shepherd.

The actuality and understanding of the verse become more vivid as we pulverize the scripture or thought. We think on it, ponder it, and allow the idea to become alive to us and within us. Lord, let the words of our mouths, the thoughts of our minds and the meditation of our hearts be acceptable to you.

Dedicated Discipline 5

Solitude – Silence is a catalyst of solitude, wherein, it relates to blessed quietness, being alone and secluded. The definition of solitude is the state of being alone, it is the absence of human activity. Moreover, solitude denotes isolation, quarantine, seclusion, and detachment from day-to-day activities. The discipline of Silence shuts out the noise of our surroundings and the people who make the noise. When practicing solitude, we intentionally remove ourselves from outside influences, society, obligations, and responsibilities. We are alone with God free of distractions, where we discover new strength; we are in a place of dependence, renewal, rest, and restoration.

We find in Scripture that Jesus practice solitude often when He would withdraw to a lonely place and pray. In Matthew 14:23, Jesus dismissed the crown and went up the mountain by himself to pray. Solitude was also being practiced when Jesus spent forty days in the dessert, prior to the start of His ministry. (Matthew 4:1-11) Again, Jesus was alone, withdrawn from the crowd, spending time alone with His Father in the garden of Gethsemane, totally involved in an intimate conversation of prayer.

Many years ago, I experienced a rewarding time of solitude, when I closed myself up in my room, fasting, praying, studying, worshiping, journaling, and hearing God for forty days. It was just God and me! I ate on meal a day when it was delivered outside my door at 6:00 p.m. I had no contact with family, church members, businesses, or anyone outside my room. God gave me instructions daily, fed me spiritual food, and poured deep revelation knowledge into me daily. This practice of solitude was one of the most spiritually beneficial and rewarding times in my life.

In solitude, there is no clutter and no struggle to hear God: all distractions and disruptions must remain silent. Understand, solitude is an intimate time of transparency before God, it is a time of fulfillment and private devotion. During the practice of solitude, our loneliness is covered by His shadow and our needs are satisfied by His presence because He alone is our focus.

Normally, our daily schedule of activities does not include time marked for silence or solitude, therefore, time must be carved out and reserved for it; the private, personal, and passionate time alone with God which must be free of potential distractions. To successfully practice this discipline, it is necessary to plan our space, place, and time to be alone with God in a judgment-free atmosphere. The time alone with God is time in the presence of pure love; moreover, this time will enhance our intimacy with Him.

Come away my beloved and spend a time of solitude with the Almighty! He longs to share intimate and quiet time with us, a time of seclusion and separation, a time of disengagement and disconnection from outside influences, and a private time to be nurtured by God himself.

Dedicated Discipline 6

Service has a dual purpose; we serve to help others, as well as, helping ourselves in a variety of aspects. The meaning of service is to render assistance or active serving, to be favorable and suitable. It is showing kindness and charitable giving. Also, it means to contribute, and to provide with supply. The greatest definition of serve is to do for and to give to. This definition encompasses the discipline of serving and giving. Giving means to impart, furnish, provide, or put forth. It is difficult to give without service and to serve without giving. Jesus was a servant who came to serve and to give. Matthew 20:28 declares "Your attitude must be like my own, for I, the Messiah, I did not come to be served, but to serve, and to give my life as a ransom for many."

The practice of the dedicated discipline of Service is to serve others in various formats that will give strength in areas of weakness. I love to serve, and I greatly enjoy giving to meet the needs of others. I practice finding the needs of others; then I secretly meet the needs. My joy in giving is in supplying and meeting the needs of others.

Service is meeting the present need of individuals, moreover, this act of service is often manifested in tangible giving. The motivation for service is: 1) Gratitude – service is the right response to God's goodness to us. 2) Gladness – we serve because of the gladness of heart and not grudgingly. We are to serve the Lord with gladness. 3) Love – We love God, and we love others, therein, is our pleasure to serve and to give.

The desire to serve is born out of a humble heart of love and strength. Consequently, the Bible says, in all we do, we are to do it in love. It is important to know we serve to give, and give to serve; and that brings glory and honor to God. We receive an abundance of joy when we render service to those in need or when we give to meet a need.

The discipline of Giving is motivated by our gratitude for God's generosity and grace. Many times, giving is a sacrificial act, and thereby can be a challenge for us. When our giving is at an uncomfortable level for us, God will be seen. We give because it is right to give as we obey God in our giving. I am reminded of the time I was instructed to get my car fixed and give it away. I obeyed the Lord's instructions explicitly and what a joy it was! I was tremendously blessed in return from that act of obedient giving. The Bible tells us in Luke 6:38: "give, and it will be given to you. Good measure, pressed down, shaken together, running over, will be put into your lap. For with the measure, you use it will be measured back to you." Serving and giving will push us past our selfish nature and allow us to demonstrate God's love. God will honor our service and our giving by blessing and increasing our resources, which will position us to always be in the position to bless others.

Chapter Three

UNCONDITIONAL YES

*Whatever God has promised gets stamped with the Yes of Jesus. In him,
this is what we preach and pray, the great Amen, God's Yes and our
Yes together, gloriously evident. God affirms us, making us a sure thing
in Christ, putting his Yes within us.*
(II Corinthians 1:20-21a, The Message Bible)

The three-letter word yes is very powerful and is one of the
success keys to our relationship with God. There are many
hidden truths found in the etymology of the word yes;
moreover, when yes is unconditional, it is more powerful and
efficacious. It is imperative to give God an unconditional yes
to His calling, His guidance, directions, and instructions. Our
yes says we agree, and our response has no restrictions, even
though we may not understand. An unconditional response
will activate and release the power of God; as well as enhance,
enrich, and enlighten our ministries and personal lives. Let us
keep the truth of God ever before us; God is omnipotent,
meaning He is all powerful, and His power is boundless,
infinite, unlimited and potent. This is "yes power" which will
restore, rebuild, revive, renovate, revamp, and repair.

The factual knowledge of who we are, whose we are and where we are in God is exceptionally important, especially regarding submitting a "yes Lord" to Him. First, we are born-again believers who have been adopted into the family of God, and we have been redeemed by the blood of Jesus…. that is who we are! Secondly, God himself has handpicked us, put His "yes" in us and has personally chosen us to be His own…. that is whose we are! Thirdly, we have been made to sit in heavenly places in Christ Jesus, which is the center of God's operations and that is where we are. God's yes within us has affirmed us as His own, in addition, our redemption and reconciliation have been sealed by the Holy Spirit of Promise.

The awareness of who, whose and where we are gives us deeper guarantees that our "unconditional yes" will not fail. It cannot fail, due to the fact it is God's yes and our yes laboring together. The foundational scripture text of this chapter in II Corinthians 1: 20-21a (The Message Bible) "Whatever God has promised gets stamped with the Yes of Jesus. In him, this is what we preach and pray, the great Amen, God's Yes and our Yes together, gloriously evident. God affirms us, making us a sure thing in Christ, putting his Yes within us." God's yes and our yes is gloriously effective by reason of the combustible and supernatural power of God. Also, God's yes and our yes together causes a power surge, activates a release of power, actuates movement of the supernatural, and produces signs, wonders and miracles. "Yes Lord"

The components of an "Unconditional Yes" are worthy of a more intense review with definitions and explanations. Unconditional, means absolute, unqualified, unrestricted, and complete. Unconditional also means definite, decisive, and determinate: without limits, boundaries, or rules, and is not subject to stipulations or conditions of any kind. To know and understand the definition of unconditional, sheds a brighter light on God's unconditional love, as well as the many unconditional promises in the scriptures. The principals of unconditional are sure and work extremely well with the little word yes. When unconditional is attached to yes, activity in the spirit realms began, the power of God is stirred, answers are released, and blessings begin to flow. An unconditional yes will absolutely release different dimensions of God's power in your life and for your spiritual victories.

Yes, is an affirmative and joyful expression, a positive and precise reply, and a function to express assent, agreement, acceptance, and approval. Moreover, when saying yes to God, we are agreeing with Him, we assent to His will, we are in acceptance of His Word and agree with His way. The combined definition of an unconditional yes will offer a clearer view of understanding the efficacy of the words and a submerged comprehension of the same.

COMBINED DEFINITIONS:

An "Unconditional Yes" means to agree with an affirmative response to God and His Word having no restrictions, no limitations, no hesitations, and no rules; and even without understanding. It means to assent and approve of His Word and His Will completely genuinely and categorically.

When we give a personal "unconditional yes" we are saying, "Lord, we are in total agreement with your plans and instructions with no restrictions, qualifications and with no conditions. What is being said is "Yes to His will, His word, and His way; yes, yes, yes Lord!" Therefore, it is yes without the need for an explanation or qualification from our Father God. We yield without questions accepting the biblical principles in His Word because we trust Him. The words of the song states clearly what an unconditional yes is:

"YES, LORD YES"

I'll say yes, Lord, yes
To your will and to your way
I'll say yes, Lord, yes
I will trust you and obey
When your Spirit speaks to me
With my whole heart I'll agree
And my answer will be yes, Lord, yes!

When God calls us to change our venue for Him or He gives us a vision of change, shares a deeper revelation of His heart for our assignments, or He gives us additional instructions; our response should be one of approval and pleasure. The examples of hearing from God are opportunities to say, "Yes Lord". Accepting the instructions are important, however, obeying them are significantly more important.

The biblical account of Noah and his encounter with God gives us a wonderful view of what an unconditional yes looks like, coupled with obedience. Noah was righteous and blameless among the people of his time; furthermore, he walked faithfully with God in the midst of the wickedness of the human race. Also, he found favor in the eyes of the Lord he so dearly trusted.

In one conversation with Noah, God repented having ever made man and the world, and decreed to destroy them both. In Genesis 6 God says to Noah, "So make yourself an ark of……This is how you are to build it…." Noah's unconditional yes to God, in, "Noah did everything just as God commanded him." He did not question or debate the instructions; however, he listened carefully and complied with every detail. An unconditional yes coupled with obedience with God's plan, gave Noah the strength to successfully complete the task. This principle of an unconditional yes will also work for us to complete our God-given assignments we have been given.

In the story of Abraham, who was the Father of Faith and the Father of the Nation, we find another perfect example of an "unconditional yes" being given to Jehovah. As difficult as the instructions seemed, and probably not totally understood, Abraham did not hesitate to act after receiving directions from God. In the book of Genesis 22:1-2: "Sometime later God tested Abraham. He said to him, "Abraham!" "Here I am," he replied. Then God said, "Take your son, your only son, whom you love—Isaac—and go to the region of Moriah. Sacrifice him there as a burnt offering on a mountain I will show you."

In summary of Genesis 22:1-13, Jehovah gave Abraham instructions and directions to take his only son, whom he loved and offer him as a burnt sacrifice on a mountain that would be revealed to him later in the journey. Early the next morning, without any questions or noticeable hesitations, Abraham prepared, packed, and left on his assignment. Immediate obedience is an unconditional yes! Three days into their journey, Abraham made profound statements of faith to his servants. In verse five, "He said to his servants, "Stay here with the donkey while I and the boy go over there. We will worship and then we will come back to you."

Abraham and Isaac departed for the mountain top, upon which Isaac was to be offered on an altar of wood as a sacrifice. Not once did Abraham question the instructions he had been given, nor did he hesitate or make an inquiry of the Lord for clarity. In fact, he carried everything with him that was needed to complete the task. Even when Isaac questioned about the absence of the sacrificial animal, his father's faith stood and passed God's test. Jehovah Jirreh provided a ram caught in the thicket for the sacrifice. From that time forward the place on

Mount Moriah was named "The Lord Will Provide". The unconditional yes given to Jehovah released power that captured the ram and magnified Abraham's reverence, trust, and faith in the God he loved and served. It is imperative that you and I trust and obey God, give Him an unconditional yes like Noah, Abraham, Jacob, Joshua, and Isaiah, just to name a few.

Spiritual dispositions of an unconditional yes are worthy of a deeper examination which will give structure for personal life application. Spiritual dispositions are prevailing tendencies of one's spirit; the physical inclination or a characteristic attitude of a matter and the state of mind regarding something. In our humanity, to trust is a physical inclination or can be a prevailing tendency because of life experiences. Trust is the foundation of relationships, and we must trust God to successfully give Him an unconditional yes.

We will review the disposition of trust, which means to rely and lean on, it also means a confident expectation, reliance, and surety. This disposition was clearly detected in the stories of Noah and Abraham stated in previous paragraphs. The Bible says to trust in the Lord with all thine heart, and lean not to our own understanding, but in all our ways acknowledge God as God, rely on and trust Him. Moreover, we are to give God a trusting yes, a confident yes which is unconditional. God is our Father, He is in control; and our trusting obligation is to have credence, certitude, and certainty in our God.

The biblical story of God calling Samuel is a perfect example of giving a trusting yes to the Lord. In I Samuel Chapter, the Lord called Samuel by his name three different times. On the third call, Eli instructed Samuel how to answer because Eli perceived it was the Lord beckoning the young lad. Samuel asked no questions for clarity; instead, he obeyed Eli's instructions. When he was called again, the child responded as instructed, "Yes, Lord, I'm listening" in I Samuel 3: 7-9 (TLB).

Samuel was young and had never received a message from Jehovah. Nonetheless, he was obedient to Eli, to whom he ministered. When Samuel heard the Lord calling his name the fourth time, He gave the Lord a trusting yes without the knowledge or the understanding of the call. Samuel's yes said, "I am listening, I trust you and I will obey you". Whenever our names are called, we are required to respond to the Lord the same as Samuel, and give God a trusting, confident yes.

The Almighty God has charted the course of our lives; He made the plan for us, now we must rely on His power to execute the plan and purpose for us. Blessed are we, if we make the Lord our trust! To make God our trust means we rely on Him, our confidence is in Him, and that all things will work together for our good because we have been called according to His purpose. It is essential we confidently lean on the Lord, give Him an unconditional yes, which positions us to be receivers of His blessings, answers to prayers and activation of His power in our lives.

A trusting yes to the Lord is indicative of our confidence in His ability and strength to come to our aid. In addition, we willingly give a trusting yes to the Word of the Lord, because God watches over His Word to bring it to fruition. The spiritual disposition of a trusting yes to God, will stimulate movement in the spirit, it will change difficult circumstances, alter situations, and remove the weight of burdens. We can rely on and be confident in God's power, which will revive, restore, and refresh. Just give the Lord a trusting yes!

The following is an exercise that will increase our trust level and position us to effectively give a trusting yes to the Lord. The scriptures on trust below have been carefully selected for

1) Meditation – engage in continued thought and reflection deliberately, 2) Contemplation – give continued attention, consider thoroughly, and 3) Pulverizing – reduce by pounding, grinding, repeating. The scriptures will energize your faith, increase your trust in God and His power. Say the scripture over and over, change the order of the wording while the meaning remains the same.

THE EXERCISE:

1. Read the scripture aloud three times. Scriptural translation of your choice or the one already provided.

2. Meditate on the scripture for two minutes.

3. Contemplate on the scripture for two minutes.

4. Say the scripture or parts of it over and over for one minute.

Proverbs 3:5-6 (NCV)
"Trust the Lord with all your heart, and don't depend on your own understanding. Remember the Lord in all you do, and he will give you success."

Joshua 1:8 (NASV)
"This Book of the Law shall not depart from your mouth, but you shall meditate on it day and night, so that you may be careful to do according to all that is written in it; for then you will make your way prosperous, and then you will achieve success."

Psalm 56:3-4 (TLB)
But when I am afraid, I will put my confidence in you. Yes, I will trust the promises of God. Since I am trusting him, what can mere man do to me?

Jeremiah 17: 7-8 (ESV)

"Blessed is the man who trusts in the Lord, whose trust is the Lord. He is like a tree planted by water, the sends out its roots by the stream, and does not fear when heat comes...."

Isaiah 41:10 (ESV)

"Fear not, for I am with you; be not dismayed, for I am your God; I will strengthen you, I will help you, I will uphold you with my righteous right hand."

Psalms 91: 1-2 (NCV)

"Those who go to God Most High for safety will be protected by the Almighty. I will say to the Lord, "You are my place of safety and protection. You are my God and I trust you."

Psalm 91:11-16 (NCV)

"He has put his angels in charge to watch over you wherever you go. They will catch you in their hands so that you will not hit your foot on a rock. You will walk on lions and cobras; you will step on strong lions and snakes. The Lord says, "Whoever loves me, I will save and protect those who know me. They will call to me, and I will answer them. I will be with him in trouble; I will rescue and honor them. I will give them a long, full life, and they will see how I can save.

The Word of God will fuel our trust declarations, confessions, as well as our personal prayers, petitions, and supplications. It is imperative to spend time studying, meditating, and then applying the spiritual disposition principles of an unconditional yes. Remember what the Bible says in Psalms 37:3-5 (The Passion Translation): "Keep trusting in the Lord and do what is right in his eyes. Fix your heart on the promises of God, and you will dwell in the land, feasting on his faithfulness. Find your delight and true pleasure in Yahweh and he will give you what you desire the most. Give God the right to direct your life, and as you trust him along the way, you'll find he pulled it off perfectly". Keep trusting with a fixed heart and give God an unconditional yes, a trusting yes to life choices, decisions, and directions. His power will be released in our favor.

Spiritual dispositions are valuable to the success of our spiritual growth and needed for our maturity in the things of the Lord. However, the disposition of trust is most significant to our growth, maturity, and the release of God's power in our lives from an unconditional yes. We must trust God, rely on Him, be confident in Him and willingly give Him an unconditional yes! Trust may be difficult at times; however, it is imperative that we put forth the effort and accept the assistance of Holy Spirit. The immediacy and frequency of giving God an unconditional yes is important, even though there are complications. The words of the hymn tell us to trust and obey, there is no other way to be happy in Jesus, but to trust and obey.

Love God, give Him a yes, obey His word, give Him a yes, trust God and His word and give Him an unconditional yes. God in turn will release and activate His power in our lives.

Chapter Four

DIMENSIONS OF GOD'S POWER

And what is the exceeding greatness of his power to us-ward who believe, according to the working of his mighty power, Which he wrought in Christ, when he raised him from the dead, and set him at his own right hand in the heavenly places, Far above all principality, and power, and might, and dominion, and every name that is named, not only in this world, but also in that which is to come. Ephesians 1:19-21 (KJV)

God is Omniscient – He is preeminent and infinite in knowledge. God is Omnipresent – He is everywhere and in all spaces all the time. Most importantly and for the following discourse, God is Omnipotent – He is supreme and unlimited in power. God is all-power and all-powerful. The power of God is the supernatural force and energy that emanates from Him. Descriptively, His power is efficacious, compelling, energetic, capable, potent, and has unlimited capacity to control and accomplish anything and everything.

The power of God is dimensional having measurable length, height, and depth; moreover, His power has no boundaries and no limitations. The measurability of dimensions was set and contained within the sovereign God who laid the foundation before creating man. Nonetheless, His power is efficacious, compelling, supreme, and absolute! The next few chapters will be dedicated to the enlightenment and enhancement of our knowledge and understanding regarding portions of the dimensionality of God's power, how we can access and activate this great power. Unfortunately, the study and research of His power is so enormous and inexhaustible, we could never capsulize it in its entirety in one book. However, a selection of Greek words has been chosen which mean power and have significant effects in our lives: I refer to these words as "power words".

The Old Testament concepts of the power of the Almighty God, has charted and recorded historical events that are the foundational truths and preparation for the New Testament. In the Old Testament, the worlds were created by the power of God's spoken words. The waters of the Red Sea were held up by the power of Jehovah, east winds blew by His power to dry the ground to allow the Israelites to cross over on dry ground. The power of God released the waters of the sea to drown the Egyptians.

Moreover, same power that sustains the world is God's supernatural power that controls and effects everything including our salvation, rescue, and deliverance. Saving power, (dynamia) which originated from God, has liberated us from the clutches of darkness; and by His saving power we have been placed into the kingdom of His dear Son and given authority (exousia) to represent Him in the earth. Redemption is by the power of the Sacrificial Lamb who died and by the power of His Blood that was shed on Calvary.

There is a substantial concept about His power and given blessings in II Peter 1:3-4 (NCV) says: "Jesus has the power of God, by which he has given us everything we need to live and to serve God. We have these things because we know him. Jesus called us by his glory and goodness. Through these he gave us the very great and precious promises. With these gifts you can share in God's nature, and the world will not ruin you with its evil desires." God is Omnipotent!

The scripture used as the chapter text; Ephesians 1:19-21 is a one of the most power-packed verses in the Bible because it is filled with more than five words for power. In this choice of scripture, we can see different dimensions of power.

"And what is the exceeding greatness of his (1) power to us-ward who believe, according to the working of his (2) mighty (3) power, Which he wrought in Christ, when he raised him from the dead, and set him at his own right hand in the heavenly places, Far above all principality, and (4) power, and (5) dominion, and every name that is named, not only in this world, but also in that which is to come:"

The definitions of the "power words" clearly highlight dimensions of God's power that are available to us, will work effectively for those who believe and activate their faith with an unconditional yes to the power.

Power – *Dynamis*	is achieving and explosive power demonstrating the dimension of exceeding greatness if we believe.
Mighty – *Kratos*	means strength, multiplying and prevailing power that is the working of His might and ability.
Power – *Iskus*	is the energizing force and strength that raised Jesus from the dead. Iskus is resurrection power.
Power – *Exousia*	is delegated authority over principalities.
Dominion – *Kyriotes*	means rulership, lordship and mighty one with authority now and in the world to come.

The scripture in Ephesians is a prayer, written by Paul for the Body of Christ's intellect, improved knowledge, and wisdom about Jesus. He also prays for our discernment regarding the immeasurable greatness of God's power made available to us through faith, which is the same mightiness and strength that raised Jesus from the grave. In addition, the above verses are the lifeline of power, hope, authority, and ability for every believer. All the actions of strength, force, authority, and rulership are a result of dynamis and exousia power, which God conferred upon Jesus, the Christ. God anointed and consecrated Jesus with the Holy Spirit; strengthened Him with might in His inner man and placed within in Him resurrection power and immeasurable abilities to activate His ministry. The Word says that Jesus went about doing good healing and working miracles. (Acts 10: 38 AMP and TPT) The mighty works of Jesus brought astonishment and praise among his disciples, who were in line to experience the transfer of exousia to work effectively for the Master. This was equipping power for the disciples who had received power by faith. For their instructions were to wait until they be clothed with power from on high. (Luke 24:49 AMP)

Jesus spoke of another dimension of power regarding the promised Holy Spirit whom the Father would send. This was a special endowment of power referred to in Act 2: 1-4, which happened on the Day of Pentecost. After the coming of Holy Spirit, which was their empowerment, the disciples preached the Word with supernatural power wherein thousands heard the message, were saved and many were miraculously healed. The coming of Holy Spirit, who is the Power of the Godhead, effected the ministry of Paul also with great and powerful signs and wonders. (Acts 4:7, 6:8, 10) That same power of God is alive, active, and available to believers today. As we submit to His will, yield in obedience to His way and trust the power of His word with an unconditional yes, we will experience dimensions of God's power.

The message from the text scripture Ephesians, is compelling as it illuminates different dimensions of God's power that is available to Believers who trust God and have faith in His Word. Here is the message of the scripture restated to include the definitions which will give a deeper understating for our application of the same. "It is ours to experience the greatness of God's achievable and able power. Being strong in faith and His might, His power will work through us. There is a level of authority that belongs to us, accompanied by supernatural power, the same resurrection power that God used to raise Jesus from the dead and then seated him in heavenly places. The authority has been given to us to walk and live in the same power and authority God gave to Jesus in honor. This authority allows us to live and work in his great resurrection power which is greater than any other principalities in the earth or heavenly realms; and the dominion allows us to rule and stand as His Representatives and Ambassadors."

We must take our seat in the heavenly realm, where there are several dimensions of power in operation. Great wisdom, revelations, and knowledge of who Jesus is has been given to the Body of Christ through the Word and through experiences of His power. The Word encourages us to allow our understanding to be enlightened, because then we will know the strength and force used to raise Jesus from the dead, which is achieving power. All these actions are a result of dynamis, the achieving power and ability of God. Moreover, His power is alive, active, and available to believers who will trust, submit and yield to God's power with an unconditional yes to the Lord.

Diligence on our part to study and meditate in the Word, then obey and make application of the Word is our responsibility. There should be a hunger and a thirst for the deeper things of God, as well as an insatiable desire to be in His Presence. These are spiritual activities that will exposes us to dimensions of His power. In addition, reading and pulverizing the Word will increase the presence of power for victories, for faith building, for healing, and for miracles. As we read the text again, prepare to utter an unconditional yes to the Word and activate the power in our lives.

The Almighty God wants to share his power with us, He longs to allow it to work in and for us; however, we must believe, we must trust Him and the working of His mighty power. We would do well to read it again for the first time and to pulverize the word of the verses in Ephesians1:19 and 20, from the Amplified Translation. The eyes of our understanding will be enlightened as we read it and believe it: "And [so that you will begin to know] what the spiritual] power is in us who believe. These are in accordance with the working of His mighty strength which He produced in Christ when He raised Him from the dead and seated Him at His own right hand in the heavenly places," The power, His power, exousia is "in us who believe"! Unequivocally, His supernatural power is in those us who believe. That is a powerful message.

To understand the deeper things of God and how to activate the various dimensions of His power requires yieldedness, which precedes from an obedient heart and the giving of an unconditional yes. Yieldedness is the absence of resistance and restraint, it positions us to activate the power as we agree, asset, and affirm the His Word. The dimensions of His power are available to us who believe; and we have been given the authority and ability to release and activate His wonderful and awesome power.

Power Word 1 - EXOUSIA

This word means permission, authority, dominion wonderful, unlimited ability and right. It denotes the power to decide, physical capability to do something, as well as a divinely given right and authority to carry out an action. Most of the references used will be from the New Testament. However, many references regarding the kingly power are in Daniel in the Old Testament. When exousia was introduce in the book of Daniel 4:17 as God's power, it clearly expressed the concept of God's unrestricted sovereignty; whose very word is power.

The concept of exousia in the New Testament is 1) the power to decide, 2) the decision to take place in ordered relationships and 3) the divinely given authority to act. Jesus empowered with exousia from his Father and made the decision to work and minister in His authority knowing it would bring glory to His Father. Yet throughout Scripture His authority and supremacy were constantly questioned. When Jesus began teaching the crowd that gathered on the Mount of Olives, He spoke with great wisdom, authority, and in parables that men had not heard before, therefore, they were amazed at His teaching. They had never heard anyone speak with that level of authority (exousia), even their teachers of the law. (Matthew 7:28-29)

Our Lord Jesus further demonstrates the authority (exousia) given to him when he forgave the sins of and healed the paralyzed man in Matthew 9:6. We are so thankful He has the power to forgive our sins. We are forgiven, accepted and empowered to be sons of God, and joint heirs with Jesus Christ. Forgiveness and acceptance are the beginning of a valid and authentic relationship with the Lord Jesus by His grace and power. Exousia clearly highlights the Lordship of Jesus.

God empowered Jesus with exousia; then Jesus conferred authority (exousia) upon His disciples to take action. This right and authority would assist them in fulfilling the great commission; as well as, completing the work of the Kingdom. All Believers are the recipients of this authority or enablement from Jesus according to John 1:12-13 (KJV) which tells us all who receive Him, accept Him as Lord and Savior will be given enablement (exousia) to become sons of God, not by flesh or the will of man, but by the will of Almighty God.

Rarely, is power and authority the highlight of the scripture in Matthews where we find the words of the "great commission" given by Jesus to the Body of Christ. However, it is absolutely first and foremost important because God authorized and commanded Jesus with the charge to commission believers to represent him in the earth by making and teaching disciples. Matthew 28: 18-20(AMP) "Jesus came up and said to them, "All authority (all power of absolute rule) in heaven and on earth has been given to Me. Go therefore and make disciples of all the nations [help the people to learn of Me, believe in Me, and obey My words], baptizing them in the name of the Father and of the Son and of the Holy Spirit, teaching them to observe everything that I have commanded you; and lo, I am with you always [remaining with you perpetually—regardless of circumstance, and on every occasion], even to the end of the age."

We are commissioned and authorized to work – the action words are "go, train, mark, and instruct. A significant question here is: How will the commission be accomplished? And the answer is: By exousia, the power and authority that was conferred upon Believers to perform that action. Exousia is the authorization, permission, and empowerment to do Kingdom work which includes the great commission. We are required to give the Lord an unconditional yes to the great commission, a yes Lord by working in His love and the authority we have been given to make, teach and baptize disciples. We can accomplish our assignment because of the power bestowed on us.

Imperatively, we must assent to the supremacy of our Lord Jesus because it is in Him that we live, move, and have our being. We are complete in Him! In fact, everything made in heaven and on earth find completion in Jesus, the Christ. Every seat of power, realm of government, principality and authority exists through Jesus and for His purpose. We would do well to know and recognize that Jesus is the divine portrait and is the express image of Father God. Jesus is the most exalted one and is first in everything, with His Father. Yet He shares power, glory, and honor with us who believe because we have been personally handpicked to be his very own, to be his ambassadors to the nations and His representatives in the earth.

Instructions have been given to us for the ministry work and victorious living, either when we were called, when our purposes were assigned to us, or through the living Word. We are given explicit directions and information for success in the book of Colossians. Hear the Lord speaking and discern what He is saying regarding exousia and the Body of which he is the head. His instructions, impartations, encouragement, and directives in Colossians chapter 1:10-12 (ESV) were given from a seat of authority. "So as to walk in a manner worthy of the Lord, fully pleasing to him: bearing fruit in every good work and increasing in the knowledge of God; being strengthened with all power, according to his glorious might, for all endurance and patience with joy; giving thanks to the Father, who has qualified you to share in the inheritance of the saints in light." We are encouraged to walk worthy and bear fruit in all the work at hand, also, we are empowered and authorized because the Lord has qualified us for the tasks.

The Amplified Bible broadens this scripture for us: "so that you will walk in a manner worthy of the Lord [displaying admirable character, moral courage, and personal integrity], to [fully] please Him in all things, bearing fruit in every good work and steadily growing in the knowledge of God [with deeper faith, clearer insight and fervent love for His precepts]; [we pray that you may be] strengthened and invigorated with all power, according to His glorious might, to attain every kind of endurance and patience with joy; giving thanks to the Father, who has qualified us to share in the inheritance of the saints (God's people) in the Light." What a powerful Word! Let us give the Lord an unconditional yes to this word, yes to authority and permission to walk worthy and display moral courage. We say yes and receive the invigoration of power which qualifies us as God's people. An unconditional yes will release and activate exousia in us and over us to accomplish the ministry work at hand, to live in His victory, to win people to Jesus and restore mankind in every area of life.

Jesus is Lord! He is Master! He has been seated at the right hand of His Father in heavenly places. Dominion is power or the use of power and sovereignty over something. Lordship is the combination of authority – the power or right delegated or given, and dominion – the power or right to govern and control. The wonder and might of lordship, which is authority and dominion, has been transferred to those who believe, yield and submit to it. This dimension of exousia has seated Jesus in the heavenly place from whence he governs and rules through the believers who have taken their spiritual seat in Him. It places us above all principality and demonic forces yesterday, today and forever.

We understand God is the establishmentarian of dominion, governing authority, rule, and power according to Roman 13: 1-3. God placed all things under the rule and authority of Jesus and appointed Him to be the head over everything. We live in His dominion which denotes the right of governing and controlling; it can be territory domination and control with the authority in the earthly or heavenly realms.

This dominion and authority are clearly stated in Colossians 2:10 (AMP) "And in Him you have been made complete [achieving spiritual stature through Christ], and He is the head over all rule and authority [of every angelic and earthly power]." All that we have and who we are is in Jesus because He is the head and over all rule and authority. We are complete in Him, empowered by Him and we have been given dominion to rule in the earth and have authority in the heavenly realm. The Living Bible Translation of Colossians brings greater clarity our union and position of rule: "For in Christ there is all of God in a human body; so, you have everything when you have Christ, and you are filled with God through your union with Christ. He is the highest Ruler, with authority over every other power." Our union with Jesus affords us the blessing of experiences the fullness of the Godhead and demonstrating dominion, power and might for His glory.

Knowing who we are in Him and whose we are because of Him, our stance is strong and powerful against all principality and rulers of darkness. The dimensionality of exousia, which has been given to the Body of Christ, is extensive and all-encompassing. The trigger to activate and release the power, might and dominion we have been given is giving an unconditional yes. When we give the Lord an unconditional yes, which is to assent and agree with Him, His power is activated and released to accomplish the task at hand. The power of an unconditional yes will cause a power surge, extraordinary event, or a supernatural occurrence in our lives, the churches, and ministries. Say yes to exousia and expect miracles!

Chapter Five

POWER OF ABILITY AND STRENGTH

I pray that out of his glorious riches he may strengthen you with power through his Spirit in your inner being, so that Christ may dwell in your hearts through faith. And I pray that you, being rooted and established in love, Ephesians 3:16,17 (NIV)

Power Word 2 - DYNAMIA

The prefix for most of the Greek words that will be referred to is DYNA which means to be able. The definition is to be able and to possess ability. Also, dynamia provides the power to do something by virtue of one's ability and resources, to be capable, to possess skill or competence.

The connectivity to the power source positions us to develop and mature into the person God says we are to be. Therefore, we possess the capability through dynamia to be. Jesus said we are salt and light, this is not optional. Accepting Him as Lord and Savior, and believing He is the Son of the Almighty fulfills the qualifications of being the salt of the earth and the light of the world.

Salt is necessary for life, as it is a preservative, a seasoning, and a disinfectant. There are several metaphoric references to salt in the Bible from durability, value, purification, to loyalty. We strongly believe Jesus' statement about salt was to point believer to their work of preserving mankind, preventing decay and corruption in the earth. The salt of the earth will preserve and purify corruption and decay that is throughout the world and many of the dimensions of God's power including dynamia will equip believers for this assignment. An unconditional yes to being the salt of the earth, together with tenacity and perseverance, we can steer mankind to a thirsty place in life. Ultimately, this will draw fallen humanity to thirst for God, His righteousness and purification.

Being the light in the dark world is possible by the dynamia (ability) and dynamoo (strength) powers of the Most High. Love and grace are properties of the light of which Jesus is the source. Moreover, light speaks to the testimony of believers, illuminating and revealing the truth in the earth. As the light of the world we have the capability and ability to:

- Take light where there is darkness, beyond the four walls of the church and to those who are experiencing the dark despair of life.
- Shine together as the Church through unity and oneness. Collectively we will glow like a lighted city on a hill.
- Share our faith in Jesus Christ. Our godly lifestyle, prayers and worship will be a bright light to draw mankind.
- Live yielded to His will, obedience to His Word and trust confidently in the Lord who will always be with us.

Dynamia is able ability, which means to have the capacity for something, be able through the state of mind or favorable circumstances to accomplish the task. Furthermore, this power is the ability to handle a situation; to be capable, to have skill or competence. A portion of the scripture text for this chapter in Ephesians 3: 16 and 17 is a prayer wherein Paul prays for the believers to be exposed to God-like strength and power that are hidden in His glorious riches. The exposure to this level of power reveals the foundational source of everything, which is love. Dynamia allows us to grasp the depth, length and height of God's love, moreover, it solidifies our union with Christ as His representatives. The combination of His extravagant love and our intimate union creates the perfect atmosphere to give God an unconditional yes regardless to the difficulty we may be facing, or the choices we need to make. Dynamia is able ability!

There is an importance to understanding our capability and competency precedes from God-power. A review of Roman 15: 13 & 14 (NIV) gives us a glimpse of dynamia in action: "13 May the God of hope fill you with all joy and peace as you trust in him, so that you may overflow with hope by the power of the Holy Spirit. 14 I myself am convinced, my brothers and sisters, that you yourselves are full of goodness, filled with knowledge and competent to instruct one another." Yes, believers have been filled with hope, joy and peace by the might and power of Holy Spirit. Therefore, His dynamia empowers us with ability to successfully teach and instruct one another. Saying yes to this dimension of power accentuates our capability and competency. An amplified perspective of the above verses says the following: "13 May the God of hope fill you with all joy and peace in believing [through the experience of your faith] that by the power of the Holy Spirit you will abound in hope and overflow with confidence in His promises. Personally, I am convinced about you, my brothers and sisters, that you yourselves are full of goodness, amply filled with all [spiritual] knowledge, and competent to admonish and counsel and instruct one another." All actions from God to man or from God for man are sources of His mighty power.

This power enhances our learned knowledge and empowers us to perform, furthermore, significant blessings accompany this level of power. The Passion Translation amplifies the meaning and makes the definition clearer: "Now may God, the inspiration and fountain of hope, fill you to overflowing with uncontainable joy and perfect peace as you trust in him. And may the power of the Holy Spirit continually surround your life with his superabundance until you radiate with hope. My dear brothers and sisters, I am fully convinced of your genuine spirituality. I know that each of you is stuffed full of God's goodness, that you are richly supplied with all kinds of revelation-knowledge, and that you are empowered to effectively instruct one another." This dimension of power (dynamia) qualifies us with capability, proficiency, and competency to fulfill the will and work of our assignments; as well as equipping us to fulfill our God-given purposes.

Dynamia enables and gives the capacity for something, makes one capable with skill; this power is quite visible in the biblical account of Nehemiah's story, in the book of Nehemiah chapters one through eight. He was a passionate intercessor and prayer warrior who carried a heavy burden to rebuild the wall and the city of Jerusalem. He prayed for God's favor which was needed and a supernatural move to be put in position to lighten his burden for homeland. Nehemiah was persistent and consistent in prayer while waiting for God to answer his request.

This is a lesson we all should learn and practice – "Give God a yes, pray and wait in faith!" When the long-awaited answer comes, it will come with instructions, enlightenment, and directions. During the waiting period it is essential to be alert and aware of His promptings and take a stance of readiness to obedience. After more than one hundred days, Nehemiah received answers to his prayers with instructions.

After months of praying, the King noticed Nehemiah's countenance and inquired about his sad face. Nehemiah's response was, "Why not, when the city of my father's tomb lies in waste? Nehemiah asked for a leave of absence from his job to return and rebuild Jerusalem. His job was very important, however, Nehemiah's burden for his homeland had become monumentally important. His unconditional yes to God caused the release of dynamai (the power that enables and makes capable) and everything needed from authority, resources, skill to opportunity was given. An unconditional yes is the action of faith that precedes the answer: the unconditional yes is the activator of the power provides the answer, ability, and capability. Let's review the following statements in the second part of Nehemiah's situation wherein we will highlight the action of dynamia:

- Permission was granted to Nehemiah and the King financed the project. He had favor and the capability to accomplish his desire for Jerusalem.
- The King empowered him with authority (exousia) by giving Nehemiah letters of authority for governors on the other side of the river.
- Nehemiah was sent on his way with a few good men who were competent for the task.
- In the face mockery and opposition, the wall was successfully built.

Directions and instructions from the Lord were clear and fully obeyed: God would rebuild the wall through Nehemiah and Nehemiah would build the people through God because he was capable, competent, and confident. Absolutely a "yes man" was needed for the endeavor: Nehemiah said yes to instructions and directions he received concerning this major project. His words of tenacity and fortitude were "I am doing a great work and cannot come down to you!" He had been empowered to complete the task. In the face of opposition Nehemiah did not waver, his yes had been submitted and he was committed to complete work.

As we continue to work for the Lord, trust and yield to Him, we are to be mindful of the unconditional yes given when the task began. We may have some challenges along the way, and we may even have disappointments, delays, or denials. Moreover, our assent and agreement with Lord's plans for our lives will require praying and waiting, waiting, and praying, just as Nehemiah did. It is significant to know once the power is released by our yes, answers are on the way, help is on the way, and we will be capable to accomplish the will and work of the Lord by His power.

Life has taken most of us, if not all of us to a place wherein we needed to make quality decisions or good choices, but we were ill prepared to do so. The answer for this dilemma a yielded yes, an unconditional yes to dynamia power. Yes, activates and releases His dynamia that gives us ability, make us competent, give us potential and enhances skills to make quality decisions and commendable choices. Remember, dynamia is the power that enables us to do something or to make choices by virtue of our own resources and ability.

Power Word 3 - DYNASTES

The power of dynamia (ability) combined with dynastes (authority and rule) gives us a different view of its working force in the world. Dynastes means able, to have power; it also means to be the possessor of authority. This is the authority and power of one who occupies a high position, i.e., governmental official, President, Ruler or King. This dimension of power is attributed to one who hold a position of power due to a family inheritance, estate or dynasty. The Greek interpretation of dynastes was the sense of the individual's authority, rule, and privilege to do, to accomplish something or operate in an elevated position because of their wealthy status in life. A further interpretation deals with inherited or acquired properties and possessions. A dynastic family may be known as 'royal' or 'princely': this is determined by the titles inherited by family members.

Dynasty history takes us from the Roman Empire, the Persian, Arabian, Greek and to the British Empire in the 20th Century, just to name a few. The Roman Empire was the world's greatest dynasty in terms of the years of rule and the vastness of the kingdom; furthermore, the Roman Dynasty that adopted Christianity. This adoption allowed the growth of Christianity to spread into a major world religion. The Greeks and Romans, alike assign their definition of dynastes to God as Ruler, as one with power and authority. Beyond any doubt we know God is the sovereign Ruler and the originator of authority, He is power!

When we consider God and dynasty, our religious minds couple God and Kingdom, God of the Heavens, and the Earth. However, His dynasty encompasses everything, everywhere and all who dwells therein are under His sovereign rule. The sovereignty of God is address in Psalm 135: 6 (ESV) "Whatever the Lord pleases, he does, in heaven and on earth, in the seas and all deeps." Only God can declare the end from the beginning because His counsel shall stand, and He will accomplish all His purposes. The review of the English word dynasty pierces our thought pattern with words like empire, regime, absolutism, dominion, and sovereignty. The Bible states that our God is in the heavens; he does all that he pleases. Assuredly, God has established his throne in the heavens and His kingdom rules over all. It is in Him we have obtained an inheritance because we were predestined according to God's purpose; He worked according to the counsel of His will. We are so thankful to be included in His will and testament.

We must consider the natural aspect of this power word. After humanity was created in the image and likeness of God, He gave   dominion over the earth, all its' inhabitants and over all the created works of His hands. Coupled with the authority and dominion for man to rule the earth were several dimensions of powers, i.e., ability, competency, capability, and strength. From Creation man was equipped to be successful, to accomplish the assignments, to build and rebuild as needed in the earth. God has empowered mankind to acquire wealth, property, society status, governmental authority, and ability to rule in the earth. The acquisition to obtain wealth and possessions comes from God, according to Deuteronomy 8: 18 which tells us God gives the power and ability to produce wealth. Also, remember the wealth of the wicked being stored up by God for the righteous. The power dynastes helps us in building and producing wealth; and positions us to leave an inheritance to our children and their children's children. The requirements to successfully build and attain blessings of dynastes power are:

1. Understand God knows the plan, He made it,
2. Give an unconditional yes to His plan, purpose and power, and
3. Trust him to bring His plan to fruition and for your benefit.

Power Word 4 – DYNAMOO

Dynamoo is attaining power that strengthens. This power makes strong, also it enables, makes capable and empowers. Dynamoo gives strength that makes one capable of living a lifestyle that is fully pleasing to God. We all need dynamoo, considering the distractions and disappointments, the traumatic condition of our world, the hardships and temptations we struggle against. Every believer should live a life that pleases God, a life that brings Him glory and a lifestyle that demonstrates appreciation for the many blessings of our inheritance. Therefore, a review of the word in two translations will enhance our knowledge of dynamoo and highlight its activity that strengthens our lifestyle of Godly living. In Colossians 1:10-12 (Modern English Version) "that you may walk in a manner worthy of the Lord, pleasing to all, being fruitful in every good work, and increasing in the knowledge of God, strengthened with all might according to His glorious power, enduring everything with perseverance and patience joyfully, giving thanks to the Father, who has enabled us to be partakers in the inheritance of the saints in light." Come on, say yes to that!

The Passion Translation amplifies the verses in Colossians 1:10-12 "We pray that you would walk in the ways of true righteousness, pleasing God in every good thing you do. Then you'll become fruit-bearing branches, yielding to his life, and maturing in the rich experience of knowing God in his fullness! And we pray that you would be energized with all his explosive power from the realm of his magnificent glory, filling you with great hope. Your hearts can soar with joyful gratitude when you think of how God made you worthy to receive the glorious inheritance freely given to us by living in the light."

The scripture gives us a power-packed list of blessing that are ours if we live a life worthy of God's Presence and power.

Admonishment is being given through prayer by Paul for the Colossians and every believer to demonstrated devoted love and consistent faith in Jesus. This is successfully done by the empowerment of Holy Spirit. He further encourages all to walk in the ways of righteousness, yielding to the life of holiness and maturing in the rich knowledge of the fullness of God, because this would please God. All of the above is possible by being energized with the explosive power which proceeds from His glory. His power strengthens and makes living to please the Almighty God possible. Submitting and yielding to dynamoo with an unconditional yes, and soaring with joyful gratitude by righteous living, positions us to receive the glorious inheritance that has been freely given. The Bible says we have been strengthened with all might according to his prevailing power, we are to a manner worthy of God's blessings and be thankful to the Father who has qualified us to share in the inheritance He gives freely.

After studying the collections of definitions in this chapter of dynamia, dynastes and dynamoo, along with the various scripture verses, our attention is directed to the power source within the Godhead, which is Holy Spirit. In everything in our lives, the good and bad, the ups and downs, the highs and lows, spiritual and natural there is the presence and power of Holy Spirit working, energizing, strengthening, helping, and assisting. The Bible tells us in John 16:13 that the Spirit of Truth comes, He (Holy Spirit) will guide us into all the truth, for He will not speak on his own authority, but whatever He hears he will speak, and He will declare to us the things that are to come. Some manifestations of His responsibilities regarding powers are to:

1. assist us with favorable choices,
2. quality decisions, and
3. enhance ability, capability, competency, human skills.

We confidently give an unconditional yes to Holy Spirit who activates and releases dynamia, dynastes and dynamoo to enhance our skills and improve our potential for situations and circumstances and positions us for elevations and promotions in life.

Holy Spirit, the power of the Godhead, is our Helper and Strengthener, also He is truth, grace, revelation, life, and love. He is efficient and sufficient in fulfilling his responsibility to activate attributes of God-power in the lives of believer. Holy Spirit is responsible for movement and disbursement of all dimensions of power, He is power, ability, strength and might. Our obligation is to submit, yield and trust Holy Spirit by giving an unconditional yes, regardless to the difficulty or complexity of what we are facing or dealing with. What is the power of an unconditional yes? It is the activation agent to Holy Spirit who releases God's power to cause an atmospheric disturbance, a lasting conversion, perform miracles, accredit our authority, hear, and answer prayers and solidify the life of victory with overcoming joy.

Chapter Six

ENERGY FOR DIVINE WORK

Let the favor of the Lord our God be upon us and   establish the work of our hands upon us; yes, establish the work of our hands!
Psalm 90:17 (ESV)

Now unto him that is able to do exceedingly abundantly above all that we ask or think, according to the power that works in us,
Ephesians 3:20(KJB)

For God is working in you, giving you the desire and the power to do what pleases him." Philippians 2:13 (NLT)

Power Word 5 - ENERGEIA

Energeia means energy, activity, action, operation, and working. The dictionary defines energy as the capacity for vigorous activity, also, available, abundant, or adequate power. There are several derivatives of the root word energy (energeia) that will be referred to in the following paragraphs.

God is the initiator and orchestrator of creative works (ergon), it was in the beginning that He spoke the heavens, the earth, and its inhabitants into existence by His power (energeia). Therefore, it is the work (ergon) of God whenever nature and people are referred or mentioned in the Bible.

Creation, in Genesis was God at work (ergon), His mighty acts (energeo) which included creating mankind in His image and His likeness. The energy (energeia) or activity of sound was demonstrated in God's work when He spoke and said, "Let there be…" After completing His monumental and magnanimous work of creating the world, the creatures of the land and sea, the elements of the air and everything in it; God created His Masterpiece – man! God's work (ergazomai), and His activity (energeia) included: scooping dust from the earth, shaping and forming man into His image and likeness, breathing life into man's nostrils, creating the woman from man's rib and giving them dominion over creation. Then God rested!

He resumed His work activity (energeia) in power for mankind and has given energy to man for his ultimate assignment found in Genesis 1:28(ESV) which says: "And God blessed them. And God said to them, "Be fruitful and multiply and fill the earth and subdue it and have dominion over the fish of the sea and over the birds of the heavens and over every living thing that moves on the earth." It is paramount to understand that God is power, all powerful and the absolute source of power. Regardless to the dimensionality, extensity and greatness of the energy, strength, ability, action, activity, operation, capability, and capacity, ALL PRECEED FROM GOD! His energy is incredible!

God's power as energy was the effect of Creation, wherein, the divine works (ergon) and actions of God where established. Yet the authority and dominion to rule was swiftly given to mankind. In Psalms 8, David wrote about considering the heavens, moon, stars which God set in place and refers to them as the "works of your fingers". Psalms 8: 4-6 (NIV) says: what is mankind that you are mindful of them, human beings that you care for them? You have made them a little lower than the angels and crowned them with glory and honor. You made them rulers over the works of your hands; you put everything under their feet:" Amazingly, man who was created a little lower than the angels and in the express image of the Almighty was given the authority to rule over the mighty works (ergon) of God and was instructed to be fruitful, multiply, subdue, and have dominion on the earth. The Creator God has fashioned us in His image and His likeness and has given us the tremendous responsibility of caring for His works.

Moreover, to successfully work this assignment, we must be cognizant and perceptive of the various dimensions of God's power which is the sustaining force of His activities and creative works (ergon). This knowledge about His power will give us the faith to release an unconditional yes to the Lord in acceptance of the endowment we have been given. Yes Lord, we have been empowered, authorized, and energized to oversee the mighty works of God. Our response to this incredible decision must be an unconditional yes; His yes and our yes together will activate the mighty power of the Almighty and we will be energized to do the work and fulfill our purpose.

In addition to our creative likeness, God has adopted us into His is royal family. As His children, we are heirs of God and joint heirs of with Jesus; we share in his inheritance. (Romans 8:17) This wonderful relationship occurred because of the fluidity of God's compassion, great love, and rich mercy for His creation. We have been marked in Jesus and sealed by the power (energeia) of the promised Holy Spirit, which is the deposit guaranteeing our inheritance. According to Ephesians 2:4-5 we are alive in Christ because of God's great love and

His energeo, the act of God's saving grace. Furthermore, the active energy (energes) is working for us and in us to keep us vibrant and alive with anticipation of our rich inheritance. The Word goes on to say in verses 6-7 (ESV): "6 and raised us up with him and seated us with him in the heavenly places in Christ Jesus, 7 so that in the coming ages he might show the immeasurable riches of his grace in kindness toward us in Christ Jesus." We have been seated in the center of God's operation and positioned to work for Him. In the heavenly realm where we are seated, is direct access to God's power, whether it is exousia, dynamia or dynamoo: an unconditional yes will activate any level of the power needed in our lives.

God's energy (power) – energeo, energeia and energes means the sense of activity, act, active, or action which can be seen in the work of the Disciples and Apostles in the New Testament as well as in ministry work today. Understand, it was God who worked through them (Galatians 2:7-8, 3: 5, I Corinthians 16: 8-9), by His mighty power which enhanced their works and gave stability to their ministries. In Hebrews 4:12a (NIV) it reads: "For the word of God is living and active"; God's word is alive and powerful, at work for us and in us, orchestrating and delegating change upon our utterance of an unconditional yes. This kind of energeia (power) comes directly from God working in us, for us, upon us, and with us to accomplish life goals, objectives, choices and ministry purposes. We can be assured of success in our ministry work by giving God an unconditional yes to the following verse of scripture: "Never doubt God's mighty power to work in you and accomplish all this. He will achieve infinitely more than your greatest request, your most unbelievable dream, and exceed your wildest imagination! He will outdo them all, for his miraculous power constantly energizes you." (Ephesians 3: 20 TPL) This verse is intensely encouraging as it iterates God is actively at work (ergon) in and with us; moreover, His miraculous power energizes us to do His will and His work. Stir the power from within with an unconditional yes to the energy and to God-activity because He is able and will not fail.

We will review two more translations of this scriptural account in Ephesians because its clarity and amplification of the title of this chapter, "Energy for Divine Works." In Ephesians 20-21 (The Message Bible) it reads: "God can do anything, you know—far more than you could ever imagine or guess or request in your wildest dreams! He does it not by pushing us around but by working within us, his Spirit deeply and gently within us." We know assuredly God can do anything above our highest or wildest dreams. Therefore, we need to start dreaming again and watch God move on our behalf; also, we need to imagine and paint vivid pictures in our minds of what we want and where we want to go in God, the efficacy in His power will bring them to fruition. The other translation is the from the New American Standard Bible, verse 20: "Now to Him who is able to do far more abundantly beyond all that we ask or think, according to the power that works within us," Do we want that power released and activated to produce in our lives? Of course, we do! Say a resounding yes to the energy (energeia), to the power (ergon) that is working within, and an unconditional yes to God's word and expect Him to move.

We have received empowerment, authority, and divine energy to be God's representatives in the earth, and to work for Him. How thankful we are for the energy that is available for the divine work the Lord has entrusted us with. The work of faith is propelled by power and energized by love. The Bible says in IIThessalonians1:3-4a (NIV) "We continually remember before our God and Father your work produced by faith, your labor by love, and your endurance inspired by hope in our Lord Jesus Christ. For we know, brothers loved by God, that he has chosen you because our gospel came to you not simply with words but also with power with the Holy Spirit and with deep conviction." We are called, chosen, appointed, anointed, and energized for the divine work of the Lord. What shall we say then? We shall say yes Lord to the call of ministry, yes by faith to evangelism, yes to deliverance, yes to the working of miracles, and yes to God's council who energizes and empowers us to accomplish His work and His will in the earth.

Imperatively, we must remember we are God's handiwork, created in Christ Jesus to do good works (euergesia), which God prepared in advance for us to do. Spending quality time in the presence of a Holy God will afford us the opportunity to glean from His personality, purposes, and possibilities. We can expect to mature in the deep things of God, as we work in new levels of trust and yieldedness. Let us stand in the authority the Lord has given us and assuredly take dominion in the earth as His representatives. We have been empowered to represent the Son of God in the earth with love and kindness, preach and proclaim His gospel, reconcile, and restore mankind, fulfill the Great Commandment and the Great Commission. We have been energized to do the work!

Jesus gave gifts to the church to assist in the orchestration of order and operation to work. Many believers will share in the spiritual mantel (ergazomai) of Jesus and the energy (euergeteo) of His anointing to work. The gifts are often referred to as the ascension gifts as written in Ephesians 4: 11-13: And he gave the apostles, the prophets, the evangelists, the shepherds and teachers, to equip the saints for the work of ministry, for building up the body of Christ, until we all attain to the unity of the faith and of the knowledge of the Son of God, to mature manhood, to then measure of the stature of the fullness of Christ," Verse 12 outlines a portion of the work to be done which is to equip the saints through training for ministry, build up the body of Christ, preach unity of the faith and assist in the maturity of the saints to stand in the fullness of Christ.

We are energized to prepare God's people for the works of service, until there is an unmistakable level of unity in the faith and knowledge in the Son of God. Our empowerment equips us to declare sound doctrine and truth in love, lay hands on the sick to recover and walk worthy of the vocation to which He has called us. The power of an unconditional yes activates and releases energeia (energy) to accomplish our divine assignments. We have access to various dimensions of God's power to assist with the work, we have been energized by Holy Spirit to do the work; our obligation now is to submit an unconditional yes which will activate the power to accomplish the work.

Jesus constantly reminded His followers that what they heard was from His Father, because His Father lived in Him. He encouraged them further so they would know that the works He was doing, was the Father working through Him; and all who believed in Him, and His Father would do greater works. We are to do greater works! We believe the Son is in the Father, the Father is in his Son Jesus, and we are in Jesus through the Holy Spirit therefore, we shall do greater works. What a wonderful equation! Jesus said whatever we ask in His name, He will do it to bring glory to the Father. We have been chosen to do greater! Love has been poured into our hearts by the Father, we have been personally handpicked to be His own, we are now in the heavenly seat of power and authority, and we are equipped and energized to do greater works for His glory. Our yes and His yes are all together gloriously effective as we work to win people to Jesus, reconcile the lost and unbelievers, and restore mankind in every area of life. Our unconditional yes will reveal greater glory, God's greater glory and His power! We will remain confident in the guidance of Holy Spirit as we submit an unconditional yes to godly activity (energeia) and doing good works (euergeteo) to benefit the body of Christ and for God's glory.

Power Word 6 - DYNADOXA

"Yours is the mighty power and glory and victory and majesty. Everything in the heavens and earth is yours, O Lord, and this is your kingdom. We adore you as being in control of everything."
I Chronicles 29:11 (Living Bible)

"Worthy are You, our Lord and our God, to receive glory and honor and power; for You created all things, and because of Your will they existed, and were created." Revelation 4:11 (ASB)

The prefix dyna means to be able, adding doxa to the prefix gives us the following definitions: the ability for greatness, the capability for wealth, splendor, favor, respect, renowned, recognition, fame, and notoriety. Dynadoxa deals with a favorable opinion which is held regarding something or someone, as well as one's reputation or honor. This is seen in John 7:16-18 when Jesus began to speak at the Feast of Tabernacle and Jesus was challenged because they could not understand how one unlearned and so young could speak with such great wisdom. Jesus quickly gave the credit to His Father saying "My teaching is not my own. It comes from Him who sent me." It is paramount to understand the sovereignty of God when defining doxa. God is very much in control of the affairs of our lives and does what He wants to, for whom he wants to and not at all if He chooses not to. Defining words such as 'the ability for' or 'capability for' fall within the realm of God's choice or His sovereignty. God has made the plan for our lives, and He will bring it to fruition according to His sovereign will.

In our lives, doxa can mean inner greatness or moral eminence. We have this power available to us for greatness, the capability for wealth, recognition, and notoriety. Our elevation of greatness, wealth and recognition is in Jesus, we are complete in Him and Him alone. Imperatively, our obedience, reliance on the Lord and faith in His word are pathways to His greatness that He willingly shares with us.

Let us reflect on the Bible story of Abram's calling and obedience in Genesis chapters12-15. He was given specific instructions and Abram was faithful to obey God and follow the instructions he was given. It was a tremendous story of faith with astronomical rewards. A portion of His reward for faithfully obeying Jehovah was greatness; his nation would be great, his name would be great, he would be the father of all peoples on the earth and thereafter he would be known as the Father of Faith. Dynadoxa was present and working in Abram's life as the favor of Jehovah was increased in his life, His obedience was the catalyst for his wealth and recognition.

The word doxa alone is extremely important and warrants special attention to acquire good understanding and comprehension. Doxa alone tends to speak to the spiritual aspect of our lives. Doxa by definition means glory, the great power of God, His radiance and His manifested presence and power. Glory is the Presence of God, the dignity, majesty, splendor, and grandeur of the Almighty Elohim. The definition of glory is the heavy laden, manifested presence of God with substance that satisfies. He brings gifts that will satisfy our needs when He is present.

Theologically, regarding believers and doxa, our exalted status of greatness and blessedness is the approbation of being in Jesus and living in His victory. An unconditional yes will solidify our union with Jesus and will position us for the fullest enjoyment of admiration and honor of God. The expression of doxa from God towards us is seen in our exaltation to a seat in heavenly places, the inheritance of His Kingdom, the sharing in resurrection power, and the enjoyment of the fullness of the Godhead bodily. It is beneficial to assent, agree or say yes to the position doxa makes available to us in Him.

The greater glory has yet to be reveal when Jesus returns. We know that the glory of the Lord shall be revealed, and all shall see it together because the Lord has spoken it. 1 Peter 4:13(AMP) tells us: "But insofar as you are sharing Christ's sufferings, keep on rejoicing, so that when His glory [filled with His radiance and splendor] is revealed, you may rejoice with great joy." When the fullness of time has come, greater glory will be revealed in honor and splendor. In the meantime, we are afforded the pleasure of sharing in spirit the doxa of God. We share in His life, His blessings, and the oneness with His Father. The Scripture in Colossians 3:3-4(AMP) highlights this truth: "For you died [to this world], and your [new, real] life is hidden with Christ in God. When Christ, who is our life, appears, then you also will appear with Him in glory." It is significant to point out that believers presently possess this glory (doxa) in spirit by Holy Spirit. For we are progressively transformed into the image of God's dear son, going from one degree of glory to another. The Holy Spirit imparts glory spiritually, invisibly, and secretly to the soul as a foretaste of the fullness of glory to come. The blessings of glory are granted through Jesus only, by His perfect obedience, his sacrificial death, and triumphant resurrection. We should willingly and quickly say yes to the presence of glory during our transformation to be more like Jesus and our transcending to draw nearer to Him.

According to the Gospel of John 17, Jesus prayed to the Father for his disciples, his followers, and future believers regarding glory. In his prayer, He asked the Father to restore the glory He once had. Also, this scripture tells us the magnificent purpose of this level of glory which was unity. A review of this scripture in at least two translations will assist us in understanding this portion of the prayer of petition and the discourse on glory offered by Jesus. In John 17: 22-24 (NIV) it reads: "I have given them the glory that you gave me, that they may be one as we are one— I in them and you in me—so that they may be brought to complete unity. Then the world will know that you sent me and have loved them even as you have loved me. Father, I want those you have given me to be with me where I am, and to see my glory, the glory you have given me because you loved me before the creation of the world. The glory that was shared was for unity; so, the Body of Christ could be one with Jesus as He is one with His father." Jesus' time on earth was nearing its end when he prayed several petitions in chapter 17 of the gospel of John. He had successfully done the will of his Father and was preparing for His return to Him. Even though Jesus knew death was forth coming, He took time to express His concern and love for the future of those He loved and was preparing to leave.

The amplified version gives us a deeper understanding : "I have given to them the glory and honor which You have given Me, that they may be one, just as We are one; I in them and You in Me, that they may be perfected and completed into one, so that the world may know [without any doubt] that You sent Me, and [that You] have loved them, just as You have loved Me. Father, I desire that they also, whom You have given to Me [as Your gift to Me], may be with Me where I am, so that they may see My glory which You have given Me, because You loved Me before the foundation of the world." (John 17: 22-24 AMP) The Lord submitted a heart-felt prayer to the Father on behalf of those who had become His disciples and had worked with the ministry for three years. Jesus knew that unity would be a key component of their success; moreover, He knew the necessity for tangible glory. The purpose for the glory was to unite and empower everyone to work diligently until He returns. Jesus was very aware of the uniqueness of oneness that would assist in the accomplishment of ministry assignments and life purposes because of His experience of oneness with His father.

Doxa can denote reputation or power. Jesus came in the splendor of His Father and was referred to as the radiance of God's glory. He was the exact imprint of God's nature and the express image of the Father according to the book of Hebrews. Jesus sought no reputation for himself because He came to do the Father's will. Doxa regarding Jesus reflects all the dynamism of the relationship between the Father and Son. Jesus was raised by the glory of the Father (Romans 6:4); He is at the right hand of glory (Acts 7:55) and He is the Lord of glory. (I Corinthians 2:8)

Our comprehension and understanding of this glory will build our faith, catapult us to a yes position in Him and establish our foundation in Him. In the New Testament participation in doxa is addressed. We participate in glory through Jesus, the Christ, we are glorified together with Him (Roman 3:23), we are to enjoy the glorious liberty of the children of God (Romans 8:18), and eternal glory is the goal of our calling (I Peter 5:10).

Doxa is equivalent to kabod which is the Hebrew word for glory. Together they mean the luminous presence as a glory cloud. (Exodus 16:10) In Judaism this level of glory is recognized as honor for both humans and the divine. Regarding God, His glory is his nature, yet he shares it with rulers and those who reverently fear Him. This glory was experienced by man before the fall in Genesis and will be invested in the Messiah with the same radiance that was lost in the fall. The Word says His glorious name is blessed and the whole earth will be filled with His glory. We are admonished in the word to ascribe glory due his name and worship Him in the beauty of holiness.

We need His powerful glory, His manifested power working in our lives, ministries, and churches. Therefore, we submit an unconditional yes to His glory (doxa), to his energy (ergon), and to His power (dynamia) to be equipped representatives, compelling ambassadors and effective witnesses for the Lord of Lords and the King of Kings. Our unconditional yes to His power will position us for greater works which will be for His honor and glory. Moreover, we will be capable of accomplishing assignments, achieving our goals, and acquiring the promised blessings as His power is activated and released by our unconditional yes!

Chapter Seven

DYNAMIS – ACHIEVING POWER

For as you know him better, he will give you, through his great power,
everything you need for living a truly good life: he even shares his own
glory and his own goodness with us! And by that same mighty power he
has given us all the other rich and   wonderful blessings he promised;
2 Peter 1:3, 4a (TLB)

There is deep significance in gaining knowledge about our God, especially in the enhancement of our spiritual lives. Meditating in His Presence, studying His Word, spending time in worship and prayer, and responding to Him in obedience will intensify our love relationship with the Lord; as well as our daily walk with Him. Beyond any doubt, the intensity of our intimate relationship with God increases from time spent in His magnificent and marvelous Presence, wherein, we are strategically positioned to give Him an unconditional and yielding yes. There must be profound trust in God, wherein we rely and lean on Him and not on our own understanding; this is done with completeness of heart. Hence, trust in action propelled by faith will release power needed to work in our lives for a multiplicity of reasons.

God, our Creator and Father is omnipotent! He is all powerful, He has all power, and His powers are unlimited. Power means the ability to do or act, power is the control, command, and capability to execute and create something. Also, power is the energy to achieve regardless to the difficulty of the task. Dynamis is achieving power that assures us by the outstretched arm of God, that there is nothing too hard for God, absolutely nothing! This is a true and powerful affirmation concerning His efficacious and unlimited power. The Scripture tells us in Jeremiah 32:17 the Living Bible Translation: "O Lord God! You have made the heavens and earth by your great power; nothing is too hard for you!" God is sovereign, all knowing and all powerful: conclusively, there is nothing too hard for Him! However, in the review of the various dimensions of power, the definitions, and our responsibility to activate the powers, it is essential to understand God remains sovereign in all things. The sovereignty of God means He can do what He wants to, for whom He wants to and not at all if He chooses not to. He made the plan for our lives and will answer us according to His plan. There will be references to a large quantity of scriptures that will be contributive in developing our confidence and assurance in the different levels of God's power.

Power Word 6 - DYNAMIS

Dynamis is the most important and the most frequently used word for power throughout the Bible. The definitions are broad and deep; the usage of this level of power spans across so many areas and arenas of our lives, to include the physical, intellectual, and spiritual realms. Dynamis power means able, ability to act or produce and effect, capability of accomplishing something, strength, might, and force. Additionally, it means to be able to achieve, capable and strong. Achieving power is the force that will accomplish, acquire, and actualize the task. Dynamis power is proficient and competent in force and energy. This level of God's power is a) intrinsic, both moral and physical; b) stands in opposition of weakness; c) a spirit of strength and vigor; d) produces mighty deeds and miracles and e) full of glory and greatness.

Dynamis power gives believers the ability to have dominion over the devil's influence in our lives. Jesus stated in the Bible that all authority had been placed in his hand and He transferred that authority and power to us. This intrinsic power enables us with resisting ability to the enemy and submitting ability to God. Giving an unconditional yes which is agreeing and assenting to God, are activation words to this level of His power. After we have submitted, assented or agreed with a "yes" God releases potency, intrinsic strength, and capability to accomplish is will His will in the situation.

Dynamis is a spirit of strength, meaning a strength with vigor, above and beyond our natural strength. When we have gone as far as our natural strength can take us, dynamis overrides our weaknesses and completes the task. This level of power was in operation in the life of Abram when he was called of God to do some extraordinary things Genesis chapter 12. Saying yes to Jehovah brought him tremendous blessings, greatness and great rewards. Dynamis was at work when Abram and Sarah desired to have a child. Both were very old and Sarah was barren. It was dynamis power working with them, empowered Sarah to conceive and Abram fathered a son.

This level of power is available to the believers who trust God and willingly give an unconditional yes to the will and way of the Lord. We have not been given a spirit of fear, timidity or cowardice, but we live victoriously because we have been given a spirit of power, of love, of sound judgment and personal discipline. Dynamis power works to give us a well- balanced mind, self-control and assist in making wise decisions, as well as life choices. There are circumstances and situations that arise in our lives in which we need God's intervention and His miraculous power to work for us. Without His help, directions, guidance, and power would be difficult to succeed. But with his power, all things are possible to those who believe. An unconditional yes laced with faith and trust is powerful because it engages and activates various levels of God's power and will motivate a release of the impenetrable and super ordinary force of and from God alone. Have faith and believe, know, and recognize powers of God are available for our engagement. We engage the Almighty God in our affairs through conversations with Him, agreeing with His Word, and by practicing His presence in worship.

The reach of communication through prayer is phenomenal and extraordinary in our lives. God becomes actively involved when we pray to him according to his Word, He hears us and answers when we agree with his Word. To agree or assent with Him or His Word means to give an "unconditional yes" to God, to His word and His will. That is powerful! The Scripture tells us in 1 John 5:14, "This is the confidence we have in approaching God: that if we ask anything according to his will, he hears us. And if we know that he hears us—whatever we ask—we know that we have what we asked of him." When we communicate with God according to His Word, there is a level of confidence that answers will be received according to I John 5:14. Of course, God is sovereign, omniscient, omnipotent and omnipresent; he knows all things, he controls all power and is everywhere all the time. However, we have an obligation to ask, seek and knock; God in turn will respond to us according to His sovereign will. The Bible says everyone who asks will receive. We are instructed to pray according to the will of God, and He will hear and answer us. Also, it is important to say yes to His will, His word, and His way to receive answers. Now that is how we get God involved in the affairs of our lives.

The story of Stephen in the book of Acts: 6 and 7 warrant elaboration. In review of portions of Stephen's spiritual encounters, we can see the effects and strength of dynamis power. This power was absolutely at work in his life. "Now Stephen, a man full of God's grace and power, performed great wonders and signs among the people. Opposition arose, however, from members of the Synagogue of the Freedmen (as it was called)—Jews of Cyrene and Alexandria as well as the provinces of Cilicia and Asia—who began to argue with Stephen. But they could not stand up against the wisdom the Spirit gave him as he spoke." Acts 6: 8-10

This account states that Stephen was full of grace, which is divine blessing and favor, also, he was full of power (dynamis) which was defined as ability and strength. The fact that Stephen had performed a great number of astonishing signs, wonders and miracles among the people, caused the supreme council to be extremely upset with him. What the accusers did not know or understand was the strength component of dynamis. This spirit of strength goes beyond the individual's strength. It means when we have gone as far as we can go in our human strength, the ability and spirit of strength (dynamis) completes the task with a supply of power.

When the council confronted Stephen to argue with him, he was empowered by Holy Spirit with remarkable wisdom in every answer and they could not refute his responses. After those against Stephen had spread many lies and false accusations, he was brought before the supreme council by force. Even though Stephen was facing persecution and death, he delivered a sermon to his accusers with dynamis power which gave him strength over his enemies and strength to face eminent death.

In Acts 7:54-60 in the Passion Translation we are given a precise description of Stephen's extraordinary victories before his death.

> "When they heard these things, they were overtaken with violent rage filling their souls, and they gnashed their teeth at him. But Stephen, overtaken with great faith, was full of the Holy Spirit. He fixed his gaze into the heavenly realm and saw the glory and splendor of God—and Jesus, who stood up at the right hand of God. "Look!" Stephen said. "I can see the heavens opening and the Son of Man standing at the right hand of God to welcome me home!" His accusers covered their ears with their hands and screamed at the top of their lungs to drown out his voice. 58 Then they pounced on him and threw him outside the city walls to stone him. His accusers, one by one, placed their outer garments at the feet of a young man named Saul of Tarsus. As they hurled stone after stone at him, Stephen prayed, "Our Lord Jesus, accept my spirit into your presence." 60 He crumpled to his knees and shouted in a loud voice, "Our Lord, don't hold this sin against them." And then he died."

Stephen, full of grace and dynamis power, died a victorious martyr for Jesus and left a valid testimony of achieving power accomplishments. This same power is available to believers who will give an unconditional yes to God and His power.

We are made in the image and likeness of God, our Creator. Many facets of our lives must mature to flourish in the authority and strength we are to work, walk and live in. Identifying who and whose we are, assenting and agreeing with a "Yes" will give a measure of confidence in His power. Dynamis allows us to utilize and engage our capability, capacity and potential that belongs to the Lord. The activation factor is an unconditional yes, which releases power to accomplish the task at hand. Our example to follow has been set by Jesus who gave His Father an unconditional yes to follow His instructions, ministered confidently in His authority, and understood His spiritual capacity and capabilities. We have been commissioned to walk in His authority and encouraged to live in His victory by faith. Because of dynamis, we have the capabilities and the capacity to duplicate works of Jesus. The essentiality of dynamis power is evident if we are to represent the Lord in the earth, because we are the ones to do the greater works, bringing glory to the Father.

Dynamis is effective in spiritual warfare as the Lord has given to us authority to trample over Satan's domain. The Bible assures us that nothing will be able to harm us if we walk and work in this authority. Beyond any doubt, the weapons of our warfare are not weapons of this world, but of might and power from God; furthermore, they have divine power with the capacity to demolish strongholds. When we have strongholds in our lives, we need to rely on His power to demolish them. Do you have any strongholds in our life that need to be demolished? Use the spiritual weapons of His might and ability, give the Lord a "yes" and allow the demolition power of the Most High, His dynamis power to the work. We are the victors and more than conquerors in this warfare, standing in the power of His might. On a personal note, there is no weapon formed against me that will work against me, according to Isaiah 54:17. I confess yes consistently to this word concerning formed weapons simply because of my past experiences of dynamis power working repeatedly in my life. I want to share a narrative regarding one of my business transactions; wherein dynamis power worked with me and for me. I was negotiating rental property and submitted my list of demands and the timelines that would work on my behalf. My paper was briefly reviewed, and I was given a quick no to my entire request. However, I chose to ignore their no and reflect on what the Lord had said. Finally, after the third no. I calmly said, "Yes you can do it, and this is how." I showed the financial plan I had prepared with the help of the Lord and offered a lager deposit. They quickly said yes as if they had never said no. I refused repeatedly to accept their weapon of no until they turned it into a yes. I did not waiver.

This word will work in your life just the same as mind when you give an unconditional to the scripture and do not waiver in your faith. The English Standard Bible says it like this, "No weapon that is fashioned against you shall succeed, and you shall refute every tongue that rises against you in judgment. This is the heritage of the servants of the Lord and their vindication from me, declares the Lord." We must agree with this Word of the Lord, regardless to the circumstances before us; we are standing and declaring His word with a yes and it is in the power of His might and ability – His dynamis power!

We are body, soul and spirit, and we live and walk in the flesh; however, we do not wage war in the flesh. We do not wrestle against flesh and blood, but against spiritual wickedness. Actually, this is not our fight, this battle is not ours, because it is spiritual warfare! In the Ephesians 6:10-18, Paul wrote metaphorically about the Armor of God and the essentiality of us putting on and wearing the armor by faith to protect from spiritual attacks. Listed in the Scriptures are six individual pieces and one weapon of the armor. The weapon is praying the spirit.

The weapon of prayer is direct communication with God, also, the connection for the release and activation of the various dimensions of His power. We are instructed in the Word to pray always with all prayer and supplication in the Spirit. After having clothed ourselves with the armor, we need to drench everything, our situations, circumstances, problems, and spiritual warfare with prayer and supplications by praying in the spirit. We pray in the spirit building up our most holy faith and pray with our understanding also. The Passion Translation of Scripture encourages us to pray passionately in the Spirit, and to intercede with every form of prayer constantly always. Prayer is our weapon and an unconditional yes attached to it is the pathway to all the powers of heaven for our earthly situations. Prayers will be heard; power will be released, and answers will be received.

The weapon of praying in the spirit works in other areas of our lives beyond spiritual warfare. If you really want to touch the heart of God, spend some quality time praying in tongues. Also, praising, singing and praying in the spirit or in English to God, will gives Him glorious honor and ultimate worship (I Corinthians 14:15-17). Our praise, worship and praying in the spirit are admirable to God and spiritually beneficial to the believers. Praying and worshipping God, combined with an unconditional yes is a formula for guaranteed responses.

Prayer to the Father, positions us for fellowship, communion, and conversation with God while His armor provides protection. If we symbolically put on the whole armor of God by confession or declaration and verbally give God a yes: we will stand firmly and victoriously against the schemes of the devil. We stand in His might, His strength and His ability and will be successful in spiritual warfare and in all areas of our lives.

Dynamis is fighting power, warlike power, or power of a host of warriors; moreover, it is overcoming power that gives victory especially in spiritual warfare; as well as other areas of our lives. Our obligation is to dress for the battle and obey the command to stand in the power of His might. This stance in his dynamis assures us the ability to stand and be unshakable, undeviating and unwavering. We dress for a battle that is not our fight, we do not fight in the battle! Then we submit to God with an unconditional yes and we stand in the might of the Almighty. The Lord will cause the enemy to be defeated before us and scatter him in many directions. The Lord is conqueror, we are more than conquerors because we stand in the power of His might, dressed in His armor and living in His victory.

There is a measure of authority that accompanies dynamis power. The reference of "powers" in Romans 8:38 stands for persons in authority or high-ranking individuals of might, whether they are celestials or earthly being. The point in case is that nothing, no force angelic or human, no one mighty will be able to stand against the dynamis of love and cause separation from the omnipotent God. This power can be described as vigor, potency, strength, force, virility, and even stamina. It denotes strength that is present and felt. We must remain conscious of the fact that the power of heaven is available and can be activated with a yes full of faith, an unconditional yes.

To conclude this chapter, I will share another testimony how dynamis power, achieving power worked in my life and on behalf of the church. In 1992 I really needed God's intervention in a commercial real estate business transaction. We had entered negotiations with Riggs National Bank to purchase our facility. I had very little knowledge in Commercial Real Estate; however, I had total trust and faith in the guidance from the Lord. I practiced praying about everything, natural and spiritual issues and decisions. While praying about the business venture, God asked me if I trusted Him; I said, "Yes Lord." Then I was given instructions by the Lord to ask the bank to return or credit the amount of money that had been paid to them in rent during the one year of us searching for financing. The one year of searching for a lender would not have been necessary, had Riggs loaned us the money initially. Their statements where, "We want to sell our building to you, but not loan you the money to buy it."

I shared what the Lord had spoken to me with my Broker; and he asked if I know how much money that would be. He went on to informed me that we were already in a contract and that we could not ask for that. My question to his remarks was: "Can't contracts be amended? I will ask for it because the Lord instructed me to ask."

I knew what God has instructed me to do and I had given Him an "unconditional yes" to trusting Him. How God was going to move on our behalf was up to Him. I asked because God had instructed me to ask and because Bible says that we have not because we ask not. The appointment was made to ask for $41,000 plus back to us. My Broker thought I was out of my lane and out of order as the Pastor, but I knew I had heard from the Lord; therefore, I insisted he make the call to the necessary parties and arrange a meeting. Hence, the appointment was made to ask for $41,000 plus. The dynadoxa, the power with favor and the dynamis the power to achieve, caused me to state my case to those at the conference table with profound wisdom and certainty. I had inner strength and trust in God to rise beyond my educational ability regarding real estate. I said what I was instructed to say, and God intervened. The end result was in our favor as the banker and real estate agents consented to my request. I am thankful for the favor of the Lord on my life and for His dynamis that was activated to resolve the issue. To God be the Glory!

God is faithful to His word which has no failure in it. As we expose our spirits to the various dimensions of power, submit an unconditional yes to His word, His will and His way, we will experience the release of exousia, dynamoo or dynamis power. Expect the release, anticipate the activation of power because there is tremendous power in an unconditional yes.

This power dynamis has been declared and demonstrated to the nations since the beginning of time. In the Old Testament

God activated His power from the faith, worship and the exodus of His chosen people. (Exodus 15:6 & 13,) The activation of dynamis is directly related to worship in the past and is a viable component in our lives now. Why? Worship is yes in action; worship is accent and agreement with God. When we worship, it is all about God, the one we are worshipping. Worship is a discipline that should be incorporated in our daily or weekly spiritual regiment; it will sure our foundation of love, build our faith and position us for a great power release.

Our spiritual maturity will be enhanced if we practice giving the Father an unconditional yes as Jesus did. Jesus had a 'ready yes' because his plight was to do the Father's will and to bring him pleasure. We are united with the Father through our union with Jesus Christ; moreover, we will submit and yield with an unconditional yes to His will. When different directions are added to our ministry work, or when new portions of God's will are revealed to us, we need to have a 'ready yes'! We must give an unconditional yes to exousia, which is authority and permission to move, to obey. Let us utter an unconditional yes to dynamia (ability) and energeia (energy) to work the works assigned to our hands, knowing it will give the glory to God and will bring Him pleasure.

The setups for spiritual growth and development are to: practice quite time in His Presence, lend ourselves to meditation and contemplation while practicing His Presence, study the word of God and celebrate His power and blessings through worship. We will be positioned to capitulate an unconditional yes to the Lord. His yes and our yes together will be gloriously evident as power will be activated and released for life situations and circumstances, and as His love and power will reconcile, renew, and restore in our churches, ministries and our personal lives.

Chapter Eight

EQUIPPED AND EMPOWERED

Every scripture is inspired by God and useful for teaching, for reproof, for correction, and for training in righteousness, that the person dedicated to God may be capable and equipped for every good work.
2 Timothy 3:16-17 (NEV)

But you shall receive power (ability, efficiency, and might) when the Holy Spirit has come upon you, Acts 1:8a (AMPC)

There is tremendous power in an unconditional yes! Yes, summons movement by Holy Spirit who has the capability and dynamism to activate and release God's power in our lives, for our situations and circumstances. We shall say yes to the Lord and trust Holy Spirit to activate dimensions of God's power for our cause. Understand, Holy Spirit is the power of the Godhead, He is our Helper, Strengthener, Advocate, and Counselor; moreover, He will impart truth, grace, revelation, life, and love to us. He is efficient, sufficient, and efficacious in fulfilling His responsibility to activate attributes of God-power in our lives.

Furthermore, Holy Spirit is the activation agent that releases dynamic power from the submission of our unconditional yes. His yes and our yes together will activate exuberant energy and prolific power for us to fulfill our purpose and complete our assignments. Our obligation is to submit, yield and trust Holy Spirit by giving an unconditional yes, regardless to what the difficulty, complication or complexity might be. Holy Spirit is responsible for movement and disbursement of all dimensions of power because He is power, ability, strength, and might!

We have been empowered to experience the incredible greatness of God's power through the activation and release of exousia which is power of authority. We are prepared and authorized to work the challenge of the Great Commission, wherein, we proclaim the Gospel of Jesus Christ, baptize new believers, and disciple others through training. We have been equipped to be His ambassadors and representatives in the earth, proclaim the message of reconciliation. After the Holy Spirit has come upon us, we are empowered to witness for Jesus, win the loss, restore mankind in every area of life, heal the sick, work in the power of His might, and live in His victory.

The magnificent greatness of dynamia, dynates, and dynamoo is available to us. These dimensions of power will help us achieve ministry assignments, give us strength, and make us capable representatives of Jesus, the Christ. After we submit an unconditional yes to these levels of power, there is an activation and release that takes place to empower us with knowledge and understanding that will sharpen our skills to handle tough situations. Moreover, we must be strong in faith and trust the responsibility of Holy Spirit to mobilize the energy (energeia) for divine works, and demonstrate dynadoxa, the power of greatness and blessedness in Jesus in our lives. We have access to Holy Spirit, who is our helper in prayer and intercession; He energizes and guides us to conduct community prayer walks, youth retreats, prayer conferences, worship revivals, and many other facets of ministry work.

Additionally, Holy Spirit actuates and sets in motion power to achieve our tasks to make godly decisions, and successful choices when we say yes to dynamis, which is the spirit of strength, vigor, and ability. The proficiency of this level of power is stirred to acquire, accomplish, and actualize in our lives for the work of ministry, our life purposes and God-given assignments. Holy Spirit manifests some of His responsibilities to assist us in favorable choices and quality decisions even in our natural lives, which school to attend, where to apply for a new job, which apartment or house is for us, to buy a car or not, selection of a mate or choice of the church to attend. Holy Spirit can assist us with decision making in every area of our lives.

Now that we are equipped and empowered, we must spend quality time in the presence of God through the practice of the dedicated disciplines which will afford us the opportunity to glean from His personality, purposes, and possibilities. The Bible tells us in John 16:13(ESV) "When the Spirit of truth comes, he will guide you into all the truth, for he will not speak on his own authority, but whatever he hears he will speak, and he will declare to you the things that are to come." Holy Spirit has come empowering us with teachings of truth and righteousness. Moreover, the Bible tells us in Colossians 1:9-10, Holy Spirit helps us to live fully pleasing to God according to the vocation to which we have been called, giving us wisdom, understand, and insight into spiritual things. We submit an unconditional yes to the power, and Holy Spirit activates competency and capability for our calling and assignments.

Remember, we have been equipped, empowered, and suited for the divine work of declaring sound doctrine in love. According to Ephesians 4:11-13 we have been energized to prepare God's people for the works of service, until there is an unmistakable level of unity in the faith and knowledge in the Son of God. Holy Spirit will direct us in organizing seminars, training through workshops, and conferences to accomplish the appointments and assignments we have been equipped and empowered to do. We have access to the dimensions of power through the Holy Spirit who will energize us as He helps, strengthens, counsels, and guides us. We are obligated to give an unconditional yes to the call and to the work of the Lord; moreover, Holy Spirit will activate, and release needed power to complete the duty at hand.

Accordingly, to activate dimensions of God's power, we must ask, seek, and knock. (Matthew 7: 7-8) for directions and guidance; also, we are to call on the Lord who will help us with decisions and choices. Expect answers when we pray, also, when we call for help expect Him to respond. Moreover, after we ask, seek, knock, and answers are received, we submit an unconditional yes; then Holy Spirit will release the needed power and ability for our cause.

We all have experienced times in our lives when we needed to adjust, choices or decisions. There is no need to belabor or struggle to make a choice or decision because we have a Counselor and an Advocate readily available to assist us. Importantly, we seek advice and guidance from Holy Spirit through prayer, meditation, studying the word and solitude. No doubt, there have been many times during the pandemic we reached the pinnacle of our human strength; consequently, we prayed and sought assistance from Holy Spirit. He is there to empower and fortify our stance whenever strength is needed beyond our human strength. Holy Spirit will release achieving and attaining power for business endeavors, enable us to make the right personal choices and godly decisions. Also, we can confidently accomplish our tasks and endeavors by trusting His potentiality and competency. We lean, rely on and are confident in His power capacity, His ability, and His capability to do His work.

Now, what are the apprehensions or the hesitations? Surely, greater is He that is in us than He that is in the world! The Bible says in 2 Peter 1: 3 (NIV) "His divine power has given us everything we need for a godly life through our knowledge of him who called us by his own glory and goodness." Yes, the structure of church has changed, yes, the outlook of ministry has been reshaped, and yes spiritual focuses are different; however, God has not changed! He has been constant in love and consistent in blessings. Now is the perfect opportunity to give God a yes because He has remained the same. The Word tells us He will never leave nor forsake us; and we say yes to that truth. He is immutable, He is infinite, and He is omniscient, omnipresent, and omnipotent. Our yes agrees and assents to His goodness and His greatness. He is the sovereign God and is very much in control of the affairs of our lives.

Unfortunately, in recent years, all of us have spent time away from family, friends, work, and even church. It was a lonely uncomfortableness forced on us because of the pandemic season. But now, it is suggested that we intentionally practice solitude, spend time away from the noise of the world, the influence of business and personal calamities to be alone with God. There is a profound need for conversations and communication with our loving Father through prayer. We require intimate and unrestricted worship time with God, as well as undisturbed intervals to study His Word and to meditate upon it. Moreover, the Lord will draw us nearer if we take advantage of the opportune time to serve Him with gladness and a thankful heart. Consistent practice of the dedicated disciplines will further empower us, water our thirsty souls, feed our spiritual needs, and secure our position to give the Lord an unconditional yes.

As we understand the prevailing and paramount work of Holy Spirit, and come into deeper knowledge of an unconditional yes, our relationship with Holy Spirit will mature to be more intimate. Suggestively, submitting a yes to practicing the dedicated disciplines will give us direct access to Holy Spirit and expose us to deeper measures of the dimensions of God's power. The focus of the disciplines is doing; they require activeness, animation and action. We are guaranteed spiritual growth, relational advancement, and enhancement of revelation knowledge when we engage in the discipline of Study, Prayer, Meditation, Worship, Solitude and Service. Additionally, engaging in the disciplines will activate the power of Holy Spirit to open the doorway to a plethora of benefits and blessings in our lives.

Imperatively, we have been equipped and empowered with revelation knowledge about the amazing little three letter word "yes" that activates, stimulates, actuates, and motivates the gigantic and efficacious power of Holy Spirit. There is incredible and extraordinary power of an unconditional yes! The Bible says: "Whatever God has promised gets stamped with the Yes of Jesus. In him, this is what we preach and pray, the great Amen, God's Yes and our yes together, gloriously evident. God affirms us, making us a sure thing in Christ, putting his Yes within us." (II Corinthians 1:20-21a, The Message Bible). Our unconditional yes says we agree and assent to His Word, with no reservations or restrictions to the power that Holy Spirit activates and releases to accomplish the will and work of God. An unconditional response will enhance, enrich and enlighten our ministries and personal lives; moreover, an unconditional yes is the determinant that causes action and animation of Holy Spirit and power.

Now, we have been equipped and empowered regarding the dimensions of God's potent, compelling and energetic power which is the power of an unconditional yes. The power of yes is activated and released by Holy Spirit, who is the power. Our yes and His yes together discharges sufficient power to accomplish our ministry assignments, empowers us to mature into the individuals we have been created to be, and catapults us into our God-given purposes.

Significantly, we submit a trusting yes, which is indicative of our confidence in His power for us to successfully complete our assignments. A trusting yes is reliance on Holy Spirit to fulfill his responsibilities as the effective and efficient power of the Godhead; furthermore, to release various dimensions of power potentialities needed for our directives and destiny. A trusting yes will move the power of Holy Spirit because it is unto Him that is able to do superabundantly and above our highest hope and dreams.

Understand, we have been equipped and empowered with the power of an unconditional yes; accordingly, we must realize its essentiality in our lives. Holy Spirit is the power of an unconditional yes; He authenticates our position with God, and validates us as the called, anointed, and chosen ones. Likewise Holy Spirit confirms, corroborate, activates, and releases God's power and His Presence for us, upon us, with us, and in us.

We are eternally thankful for God's firm foundation of love, which is the launching pad He created and designed for us. It is upon this love foundation that we launch ministries, complete our assignments, fulfill responsibilities, improve relationships, demonstrate obedience to God, and submit an unconditional yes to His will as we demonstrate unconditional love for mankind. Also, we share the unconditional love of God when we preach the gospel, proclaim liberty for the bound, offer salvation to the lost, and decree reconciliation, refreshing and restoration to men. From the beginning of time, God has demonstrated agape toward His magnificent Creation, loving us with an everlasting love full of mercy and compassion. We have been prepared to reciprocate His amazing love through worship, honor, righteous living, giving and service, yielding to His instructions and trusting His grace and power.

Absolutely, now would be an excellent time to give God an unconditional yes to His love call because it was His love that sustained us through the upheaval of sicknesses, deaths, and other losses, specifically during the Covid-19 season. The Word says we continually live nourished and empowered by His love; even through the pain, the tears, and the agony of grief. We are recipients of God's unconditional love, moreover, His love foundation is strong, enduring and sturdy. We have been empowered to endure the problems of life, with our focus remaining fixed on the sustainability of His agape. Consequently, because we love and obey God, we are afforded the honor of living in His love and victory.

The Father's love is dynamic and expressive; in as much as, God has poured His love into our hearts flooding us with Himself. Our expression of love is returned to God and demonstrated when we agree and assent to His word by giving Him an unconditional yes: as well as, when we obey the supreme commandment to love God with all our passion, energy and thought. An in-depth study on love (agape) will assist us to adapt to His excellent and magnanimous love, enhance our intimacy with the Lord and further empower us to demonstrate His agape for all of mankind.

Now we are ready, we are prepared, we are equipped, and we are empowered for Holy Spirit to work through us, to achieve infinitely more than our greatest hopes or desires. We stand unwaveringly on God's word and on a firmly established love foundation, from whence we give an unrestricted yes to God. Unequivocally, love is something we do! Yes, to God's love will empower us for our assignments, commitments, and endeavors; and employ Holy Spirit to actuate and release various dimensions of power for our purposes. The power of God's love is phenomenal! The experience of influential and compelling possibilities is endless because of the power of His love. Understand, we must reciprocate love to God through worship, obedience, and trust; as well as, by working the works of Him that has called and chosen us to be His own. His yes and our yes together will be gloriously evident as power is released for miracles, deliverances, salvation, redemption, reconciliation, favor, and restoration. "Now glory be to God, who by his mighty power at work within us is able to do far more than we would ever dare to ask or even dream of—infinitely beyond our highest prayers, desires, thoughts, or hopes. 21 May he be given glory forever and ever through endless ages because of his master plan of salvation." Ephesians 3:20-21(TLB)

ENDNOTES

Reference Books

Geoffrey W. Bromiley, (Translator), Theological Dictionary of the New Testament, Grand Rapids, MI (William B Eerdmans Publishing Company, 1985)

The Hebrew Greek Key Word Study Bible, New International Version, (AMG Publishers, Chattanooga TN, 1996)

Bible reference codes and the full name of the translation used.

AMP	Amplified Bible
AMCPC	Amplified Bible, Classic Edition
ESV	English Standard Version
MSG	The Message
NASB	New American Standard Bible
NCV	New Century Version
NJKV	New King James Version
NLV	New Living Version
NIV	New International Version
TLB	Living Bible
TPT	The Passion Translation

AUTHOR BIOGRAPHY

Bishop Carrie J. Surratt is Senior Pastor of The Lord's Church of Restoration in Clinton, Maryland and Founder and President of Bible Prayer Time Faith Ministries, Incorporated. Bishop Surratt has served as the Academic Dean of the Restoration Development Institute. She serves on the College of Bishops of Kingdom Fellowship Covenant Ministries (KFCM) and functions as the Bishop of Intercessory Prayer.

Bishop Surratt is a native of Alexandria, Virginia where she completed her primary education. She pursued her academic studies at George Washington University, University of Maryland, Washington Bible College, and Rhema Bible School. Bishop Surratt earned her master's degree in Religious Studies at Washington Saturday College and received an Honorary Doctorate of Humane Letters from Washington Saturday College, Washington, DC. In November 2015, Bishop Surratt received an Honorary Doctorate of Ministry from Kingdom Covenant Theological Bible College, Baltimore, MD.

Doctor Surratt has served on the planning committee for Minority Women in Ministry for the National Council of

Churches, USA. She was selected and is profiled in "Women of Achievement", the first book of history in Prince George's County, Maryland that chronicles women and their accomplishments. Doctor Surratt has been accepted and is listed in Who's Who in America, 2021-2022. Also, she is the author of the book on prayer "Lord, Teach Us To PUSH".

By due prudence and examination, Bishop Surratt was consecrated into the Episcopacy by the Sacred College of Bishops in 2001. She was further elevated in the Episcopacy in November 2004, and is the Presiding Bishop of Restoration Covenant Ministries, (RCM) of Clinton, MD, an apostolic and spiritual covering for bishops, pastors, para-ministries, and businesses.

Bishop Surratt attended The Joint College of African American Pentecostal Bishops' Congress in Cleveland, Ohio; she was an active member for twenty (20) years; and served as Secretary for the Advisory Board for 10 years. She is also affiliated with Boundless Ministries, Inc. of Maryland, and their Global Mission Ministry. She has worked in missions preaching, teaching, distributing food, clothes and medicated sleeping nets in Kenya and Uganda, East Africa, and Cape Town, South Africa.

Bishop Surratt is an anointed preacher, a profound teacher of the Word of God, and an excellent conference speaker. Her greatest desires are to win the lost, bring restoration to fallen humanity and be an effective servant to the Body of Christ for God's glory.

ADDITIONAL WORK BY THE AUTHOR

Prayer is foundational to the life of every believer. Lord, Teach Us To PUSH is a detailed book on many facets of prayer, along with what prayer offers us. A deeper understanding of the effects of prayer will give the determination to PUSH – Pray Until Something Happens. This book is readily available on Amazon.

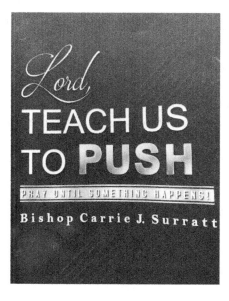

Made in the USA
Middletown, DE
26 October 2022

13495102R10066